THE NEW BIRTH

To my wife
June
with grateful thanks
for your love and support

The New Birth

A.T.B. McGowan

Christian Focus Publications

© 1996 A.T.B. McGowan
ISBN 1 857 92 241 7
Published by
Christian Focus Publications Ltd
Geanies House, Fearn, Ross-shire,
IV20 1TW, Scotland, Great Britain.

Printed and bound in Great Britain by
Cox & Wyman Ltd, Reading, Berkshire

Cover design by Donna Macleod.

Scripture quotations, unless otherwise stated are from
the New International Version
Copyright © 1973, 1978, 1984 by International Bible Society.
Published by Hodder and Stoughton

Contents

Foreword

The most amazing experience anyone can have is to become a member of God's family. It is an experience so radical and transforming that the Bible calls it being 'born again'. Unfortunately, that phrase is often ridiculed by the secular world. Just as unfortunately, the experience of the new birth is undervalued by many within the Christian church. This book will make a valuable contribution towards rectifying both errors.

It is first and foremost a *serious* book. There is no froth and bubble here. It tackles important doctrinal issues head on and seeks to unravel concepts which are usually thought to be the preserve of full-time theologians.

Nevertheless it is a *simple* book. It does not unload large dollops of indigestible theology on the reader. Instead, it seeks to break it down into the kind of language that makes it more easily accessible.

Thirdly, it is a *systematic* book. All the important doctrines involved in the experience of becoming a Christian are carefully linked together in a way which makes one marvel all the more at the grace of God in salvation.

Many a new Christian (and some not so new!)

will have cause to be thankful to Andrew McGowan
for this helpful presentation. I warmly commend it
to its readers.

John Blanchard
Banstead, Surrey
April, 1996

Preface

When I first became a Christian I did not properly understand much of what I was reading in my Bible. That is natural enough, because it takes time and effort to understand and to learn the Christian faith. Even today, almost 28 years later, I am learning new things all the time and gradually understanding the old things better. The study of Christianity is the task of a lifetime.

This book is for those who would like some help with the task. Perhaps you have recently become a Christian and want to know what has happened to you and what to expect as you grow in your newfound faith. Perhaps you have been a Christian for many years but have never had the time, or taken the time, to study carefully what God has been doing in your life over these years.

I must say at the beginning, however, that this book is not for those with a purely intellectual interest in Christianity. The Christian faith has to be lived as well as learned and it cannot be properly understood except by those who have already started on the Christian life. In other words, this is a guidebook intended for those who have embarked on the journey of faith. Those whose hobby is to collect guidebooks will not find it useful!

I have tried to make the book as clear as possible, although to get the greatest benefit will require serious thinking and careful study of the Bible. Some questions have been added as an appendix in order to encourage this thinking. Wherever possible, theological words have been explained or avoided. It is my hope that a careful reading of this book will help people go on to study the doctrines of the faith in more detail.

Having said that, however, I am very conscious of much that has not been said. There are some topics which have not been touched upon at all, and some which have only been mentioned in the passing. This is inevitable given the limited space available in a short paperback. Please bear in mind that this book is intended as a 'starter'.

The first time I attempted to write on the subject of the new birth was for a series of addresses at the Gairloch Convention in 1987. The memory of that preparation is still vivid because I was using a wordprocessor for the very first time and I went through an awesome struggle as I tried to come to terms with the new technology – with the constant temptation to go back to the typewriter! The first time I gave a series of addresses on the subject of holiness was at the Lewis Convention in 1988. A number of the chapters in this book have their origins in the addresses given at those two Conventions. I would like to record my thanks to the minister and Kirk Session of Gairloch Parish

Church and also to the Presbytery of Lewis. Without the stimulus of those invitations this book might never have seen the light of day.

Various friends read part or all of the manuscript at different stages over the past few years. I am grateful to all of them. I am, however, particularly indebted to three friends who went through the manuscript with a fine tooth comb and suggested many corrections and alterations. Without their kindness and help this book would be much worse!

First to Noel Agnew, minister of Oldpark Presbyterian Church in Belfast. A friend for over 20 years, Noel was a schoolteacher before becoming a minister. He treated my manuscript with the ruthless but fair treatment that one expects of the better type of schoolmaster. Of the three who made comments on the text of the manuscript he had perhaps the hardest job, since he was working on the first draft. Being in its infancy and decidedly rough hewn, much work was required to bring it into some kind of shape. Only his warm Irish sense of humour could have sustained him through many hard and demanding hours of unrewarding labour.

Second, to Hector Morrison, my colleague at the Highland Theological Institute. Hector's careful and rigorous eye for detail, his calm and judicious nature, allied to a wisdom and discernment akin to that of Solomon, have kept me out of trouble on many occasions since we began working together – not least in respect of this manuscript

where he spotted many potential theological pit-
falls. In addition, as a skilled linguist and gram-
marian, he pounced gleefully on every split infini-
tive or incorrect tense. I was sorely tempted to in-
clude a series of errors in this preface (which he
has not seen) just to try and get something past
him!

Third, to John Blanchard. Not only did John
kindly write a foreword for this book but he also
took the time to go over the manuscript thoroughly
and suggest numerous changes. Not a page escaped
his red pen (or perhaps, by the time he was finished, two red pens!). To have the benefit of one's
manuscript being read by an experienced and gifted
writer means more than I can say. He was constantly
pulling me up for some infelicity or other, constantly telling me to be more focused on the person
for whom the book was intended, and so on – it
was like attending a master class in how to be a
writer of Christian books led by a true master of
the craft. If, in time, I learn to be a better writer,
much of the credit must go to him.

I must also thank Malcolm Maclean, the theological editor at Christian Focus Publications, who
is also a friend and a part-time student here at HTI.
His patient understanding while I produced this
book in the midst of an extremely busy life was
much appreciated, as is his skilful final editing.

It was William Mackenzie, the managing director of Christian Focus Publications, who first asked

me to write this paperback, after I had spoken at the annual theological conference of the Associated Presbyterian Churches in Inverness. I am grateful for his interest in this work and for his willingness to risk putting it into print.

Above all I must thank my family, especially my wife June to whom this book is dedicated. Only our closest friends know how much she has had to put up, with being married to me! My lifestyle is such that there are always a dozen different projects on the go at the same time and, apart from occasionally telling me that I should learn to say 'No', she has always been very understanding. I have also spent numerous hours in front of the computer while she helped the boys with their homework and did other things which are as much my responsibility as hers. I cannot properly express what her love and support mean to me.

Finally, to Scott, David and Christopher, my sons, who have put up with their father and his many failings. This is written with the fervent hope and prayer that the subject of this book will become a reality in each of their lives and that they will grow up to love and serve the Lord and pass on this message of regeneration to others.

Chapter 1

THE BEGINNING

I remember clearly the night on which I was 'born again'.

It was the 5th of May 1968 and I was in the second year at Uddingston Grammar School in Lanarkshire. Some of my friends attended the Scripture Union group in the school, and they had begun to talk to me about the need to be 'born again'. That night, at their invitation and in the company of my next door neighbours, Mr and Mrs McGhie, I went to a meeting in the Brethren Gospel Hall in Uddingston. The preacher was an Irish evangelist called Hedley Murphy.

Partly due to what my friends at school had told me, and partly due to what Mr and Mrs McGhie explained to me as we went to the meeting, I decided to stay behind afterwards and talk to the evangelist.

My life was changed that night. There are various ways of describing what happened. You could say that I became a Christian, or that I was 'born again'. Some would say that I was 'saved' or 'converted'. The purpose of this book is to try and explain what happened that night, by looking at what the Bible has to say. Above all, this book has been written so that many other people might understand what it means to be born again.

Early Days

From my earliest days I attended church and several organisations connected with the church, including the Boys' Brigade and the Band of Hope. In my schooldays I often attended three or four church meetings every week.

My parents were heavily involved in the church, my father as an elder and my mother in the Woman's Guild and various other aspects of the life of the congregation. On Sundays we went as a family to church, and my sister and I attended Sunday School and then, later, Junior Fellowship. In addition I had the Boys' Brigade Bible Class before the morning service.

There was never a time when the church did not play a significant part in my life. Despite that, I do not remember ever hearing anyone tell me that to be a Christian an individual must be 'born again'. It may well be that I just wasn't listening carefully enough, or that I was too preoccupied with other things to pay attention. It may even be that I *was* told and simply failed to understand what I was being taught.

Be that as it may, when my Brethren friends at school began to speak about this idea of being 'born again', it came as a surprise to me. Not only had I been born and brought up within the life of the church, with my parents encouraging me to pray and read the Bible from an early age, but I had already begun to think of becoming a minister! Six months before that night in the Gospel Hall I had been sitting in a pew in my home church when I had the strange yet strong conviction that God was speaking to me, and telling me that he wanted me to become a minister. I hated the very idea! As far as I was concerned nothing could be more dull and boring. I wanted a life of action, perhaps the life of a soldier like my father, who had fought with the Argylls during the Second World War and had been a prisoner of the Japanese for several years after being captured when Singapore fell.

I fought against the idea for weeks, but eventually I came to the firm conclusion that God *did* want me to become a minister and that to do anything else would be to avoid my calling. Imagine how I felt, therefore, when six months later I had to ask myself whether or not I was really a Christian at all! The question was unavoidable. When I was challenged I could only say that I had been baptised, that I had always attended church, that my parents were Christians and so on. But there had never been anything in my own experience which could be described as 'new birth'. Yet this, I was told, was what was required.

New Birth

That night, Hedley Murphy and one or two others
(including George Hanlon, the father of one of my
Scripture Union friends) explained to me from the
Bible that to be a Christian meant to be 'born again'.
In other words, becoming a Christian was not like
joining a club. Instead, it was a supernatural experience in which an individual had a personal encounter with God. They pointed to verses in the
Bible like John 5:24 and Romans 10:9, in which
the good news about salvation was clearly spelled
out. They spoke about people who had met with
Jesus and whose lives had been changed. They told
me that if I responded to the call of the gospel then
my life would also be changed.

That very night I experienced the new birth and
my life has never been the same since. Immediately, I felt like a new person and there was a joy
and a peace which I had never felt before. Mr
Murphy encouraged me to tell someone. That night
I told my parents and also an uncle who was up
from England on holiday. A Baptist lay preacher
himself, he was particularly delighted and has been
a great help to me ever since.

Later that week I was asked to speak at the Scripture Union and give my 'testimony' which I dis-
covered meant I should tell people that I had become a Christian. It was a nerve-racking experience but undoubtedly a valuable one, and the Scripture Union from then on became a place of growth

and nurture for my spiritual life. Shortly afterwards I met and came to know Philip Malloch, the school chaplain, whose influence was most helpful and who taught me a good part of what I know about evangelism (spreading the good news to others), lessons which were expanded and deepened much later by Stephen Anderson, the Church of Scotland evangelist.

It is now over a quarter of a century since I was born again. I have spent many years in full time and part-time theological study and have served for fourteen years as a parish minister of the Church of Scotland. My current ministry involves teaching theology to students in Elgin, while continuing to preach regularly. Only now, with the benefit of study and hindsight, can I look back to that night and understand what happened. It was both simple and complicated. Simple, in the sense that becoming a Christian is a simple act; and complicated, in that God was doing something much more profound and significant than I understood at the time.

As we explore what God was doing that night and what he has continued to do, please ask yourself this question: Have I been 'born again'? If the answer is 'yes', then I hope this book will help you to understand more fully the significance and consequences of the new birth. If the answer is 'no', then I hope by the time you get to the end of the book you will be ready to come before God and ask him to change your life as he changed mine.

Chapter 2

THE NEED FOR REGENERATION

In describing my experience on the night of 5th May 1968 I said that I had been 'born again'. Theologians call this 'regeneration'. We are going to examine this doctrine in some detail. As we do so, it will become obvious that the concept of new birth is at the very heart of Christianity. In fact, as our study develops we will find ourselves drawing together many of the main themes of Christianity.

We must begin, however, by asking the obvious question: Why does anyone need to be 'born again'? In order to answer this question we must discover what the Bible says on the subject. This last point requires a word or two of explanation. I am convinced that the Bible (both the Old Testament and the New Testament) has come to us from God and so has complete authority. In other words, I am working on the presupposition that what the Bible says is true because it is the Word of God rather than just the words of men. To explain and defend this position would take too much space in this short book, but what is written in these pages will only make sense if you recognise the standpoint from which it is written. If you want to understand this standpoint better, you should read the book *God has Spoken* by the English theologian J.I. Packer [1].

It is also true that you will find it much easier to understand what is being said if you look up the passages from the Bible as they are mentioned. The version which I am using is the *New International Version*. Bible references will be given in a standard form: for example, Romans 10:9-13 refers to the Book of Romans, otherwise known as Paul's letter to the Romans, chapter 10, from verse 9 to verse 13. The abbreviation 'ff.' means 'and the verses which follow'.

The Bible tells us that every single human being needs to be 'born again' and gives two main reasons: first, because of the condition of mankind; and second, because of the nature of God. Let us consider these two reasons:

1. The Condition of Mankind

Paul, a great missionary and theologian in the very earliest days of Christianity, wrote a number of letters to different churches and individuals in which he tried to explain the meaning of Christianity. In one of these letters, written to the Christians in Ephesus, Paul paints a graphic picture of human nature. The passage in question comes in the second chapter of the letter.

---

1. Published by Baker Book House, Grand Rapids, USA.

Ephesians 2

Paul's purpose in this chapter is to remind the Ephesians of what they were like before being born again, and to describe the change which has taken place. This 'before and after' picture enables us to contrast the condition of mankind by nature with the condition of those in whom God has done his work.

Paul tells the Ephesians that before God came to them they were spiritually 'dead' (verse 1). Worse still, they were by nature 'objects of wrath' (verse 3). This means that God was angry with them and regarded them as his enemies. Paul goes on to say that they were 'separate from Christ', 'excluded from citizenship in Israel', 'foreigners to the covenants of the promise', 'without hope' and 'without God in the world' (verse 12). Taken together, these expressions tell us that the Ephesians were entirely cut off from God.

Paul then gives the opposite side of the picture and describes what they have become and immediately we see that their situation has dramatically changed. Among other things he describes them as 'fellow citizens with God's people and members of God's household' (verse 19).

Our main concern in this chapter, however, is with their former condition. What we must try to discover is why Paul described them as being spiritually dead and why he said that they were by nature objects of God's anger and judgement. Is it just that these Ephesians were particularly evil people? Or are we all the same?

In order to answer this we must go to another letter written by Paul, this time to the Christians at Rome. In that letter, Paul said that 'all have sinned' (Romans 3:23). He reached this conclusion after several pages of careful reasoning. A careful reading of these two letters, and of many other statements in Scripture, leads to one unmistakeable conclusion: every person born on this planet is a sinner.

By the word 'sinner' the Bible means someone who is in rebellion against God and who constantly breaks God's law. But why should this be? Does the Bible not tell us that God created the world and that everything was 'very good'? How then did everything become 'very bad'? In order to understand how such a situation came about we must turn to the third chapter of the very first book in the Bible. The events of that chapter form the basis for any proper understanding of the condition of mankind.

Genesis 3

Genesis chapter 3 describes what has come to be known as the 'Fall'. The first two chapters of the book tell us that God created everything (out of nothing) and that the whole creation was perfectly good. But then the first human beings, Adam and Eve, made a deliberate decision to disobey God and disaster followed. They chose to listen to the voice of the serpent (or the devil, sometimes called Satan) rather than the voice of God.

In making this decision, our first parents asserted their own independence and self-sufficiency. They were saying, in effect, that all their decisions from that point on would be made on the basis of what they wanted, rather than on the basis of what God said. That is to say, they were now looking at the world as if it revolved around them, instead of thinking out of a centre in God.

To 'think out of a centre in God' means to have a view of the world which recognises that God is the creator and sustainer of the whole universe, and that everything comes from him and is responsible to him. It is to see everything from God's point of view and to be completely obedient to what he says. This is the way it was in the beginning, as described in the first two chapters of Genesis.

The new situation which our first parents created was completely different. They chose to listen not only to God but also to Satan. Having done so, they weighed up what God had said and what Satan had said and then made a decision. In doing so they were saying something very important. They were saying that God's Word was an opinion which they would consider, rather than the final authority in all decision-making. In short, they were saying that human beings were capable of putting God in the balance and deciding whether or not to believe what he said. Do you see how serious this is? The creature had become so full of his own importance that he felt he could put the Creator in his place! Immediately, everything changed. The relationship between God and humanity was broken, Adam and Eve were banished from the presence of God, and God's judgement fell upon them. Because Adam was the representative of the human race the judgement also fell upon every human being born from then until now – except Jesus Christ (see chapter 6 for an explanation of this).

From this point on, until the present time, man has been a warped creature. He has ceased to be truly human because, having been designed to live in fellowship with God, he can only find true significance and real meaning in the context of that relationship. The problem is that, instead of living in total dependence upon God, he has now declared himself to be independent of God. Mankind was never intended to live like this, and is not equipped to do so.

On an island in one of my former parishes there was an old car which was used as a chicken coop! It was still recognisable as a car, but was incapable of fulfilling the function for which it had originally been designed and built. Mankind is in the same condition. The ridiculous spectacle of men and women who have declared themselves to be independent of their creator is as pathetic as that car being reduced to a mere chicken coop. The Bible tells us that man was made in the image of God, but at the Fall this image was defaced and his nature was corrupted in every part. It is because of the Fall and the consequent corruption and perversion of humanity that every human being born on this planet is a sinner, and is held to be in rebellion against God.

The other consequence of the Fall was that decay and death came into the world, affecting not only human beings but also the very creation itself. Death and decay were not part of God's original plan but were rather a direct result of mankind's rebellion against him.

Everything which God has done since the Fall is designed to undo the effects of that tragedy. In particular, the new birth is intended as a means of recreating us in the image of God, thus enabling us to be restored to fellowship with him.

Romans 1:18-32

If we now consider the first chapter of Paul's letter to the Romans (verses 18-32) we find one of the most powerful descriptions of fallen humanity anywhere in the Bible. This passage tells us that every human being knows the truth about God but wickedly suppresses this knowledge (verse 18). Creation, conscience and the remnants of the image of God in every human being bear eloquent testimony to the existence and power of God, but men and women, because of their sin, refuse to believe the evidence. There is, however, no escape. The evi-

dence is so clear that no one will be able to stand
before God and offer any excuse for unbelief (verses
18-20).

Since this is so, God's wrath is being directed
against all the godlessness and wickedness of those
who suppress the truth in this way. Indeed, we are
told that God 'gave them over' (verses 24,26,28).
The implication of this phrase is that God withdrew
from them completely and left them in their sin.

Although the Fall has taken place and we are all
by nature totally depraved (in the sense that every
aspect of our nature is affected by sin) we are not
as bad as we could be. God acts to prevent sin being allowed full reign, and he does this even in the
lives of those who are not 'born again'. That is why
we meet so many people whom we would call
'good' even although they are not Christians. This
is one result of what the theologians call *God's common grace*.

In the Romans passage, however, even God's
common grace has been withdrawn, and sin is allowed complete liberty in the lives of those concerned. If you want to know what sin would be like
if all the restraints of God were to be taken away,
then here is the picture – and it is a vile and horri-
ble sight. Having said that, if you read these verses
you will see that many of these practices are becoming commonplace today. To give just one example, we are fast approaching the situation in the
UK where homosexuality is regarded as a normal

and acceptable alternative to heterosexuality. Yet as far as Scripture is concerned it is a sinful perversion which calls forth the judgement of God.

Titus 3

If we now turn to the third chapter of Paul's letter to Titus, we find another example of the 'before and after' picture we saw in Ephesians 2. The importance of this passage is that it refers to the Jews. Anyone reading Ephesians 2 or Romans 1 could argue that Paul was speaking about a particularly sinful and wicked group of people and conclude that only *some* people are sinners who need to be born again. I recall a minister telling me that these chapters refer only to the outcasts of society, those who are obviously in need of God's forgiveness: the thieves, murderers, rapists, drug pushers and so on. The 'nice' people, on the other hand, the ones who 'try to do their best', are in a different position altogether.

That myth is dispelled here. In verse 3 Paul says: 'At one time we too were foolish, disobedient, deceived and enslaved by all kinds of passions and pleasures. We lived in malice and envy, being hated and hating one another.' Notice that Paul includes himself in this description of sin – he uses the word 'we' – and yet he was a deeply religious man, zealous for the things of God.

This is very important. Many people today are like the minister I mentioned. They use the word 'sinner' to refer only to criminals. The idea that a cultured, religious person who tries to live a good life is also a sinner in the eyes of God seems absurd to them, but it is true. We could, of course, look at many more passages from the Bible but hopefully the point has been made. Men and women are sinners in the eyes of God and by nature are spiritually dead.

It is vital that each of us clearly grasps this teaching about sin before we go on because, until we have been persuaded that this is a true description of the human condition, we cannot understand what genuine Christianity is all about. Christianity teaches us about the forgiveness of sins, the new birth and new life. But none of these will make any sense unless we believe that they are necessary. If we do not take sin seriously we will not have an adequate understanding of its remedy.

The main reason why the Christian message is disregarded by so many people today is simply that they see no need for it. The average man and woman in the street do not believe that they are sinners and hence see no need for forgiveness. As a result, most people do not take sin seriously. They joke about 'sin', and regard the moral teaching of the Bible as outdated and irrelevant. Yet strangely, the same people who so quickly dismiss talk of sin and forgiveness, often believe that they will go to heaven when they die! Unfortunately, they are sadly mistaken. As we shall see later, only those who are

born again and whose sins have been forgiven will
go to heaven. Everyone else, the Bible tells us, will
go to hell.

We might put it like this: the Christian gospel is
only for sinners. Jesus of Nazareth, the Son of God,
said that he did not come to this earth with a message for self-righteous people but only for those
who know themselves to be unrighteous. He said
that just as those who are physically fit do not need
a doctor but only those who are sick, so his message is only for those who know themselves to be
spiritually sick.

2. The Nature of God

The other main reason why new birth is necessary
concerns the nature of God. The Bible tells us that
God is holy (look up Leviticus 11:44; 19:2; Joshua
24:19; 1 Samuel 6:20; Psalm 22:3 and Isaiah 57:15)
and righteous (look up Psalm 31:1; 145:17; Isaiah
45:21 and Jeremiah 11:20; 23:6). He hates sin and
cannot bear its presence. Indeed, the very reason
for the breach between mankind and God is that a
sinner cannot come into the presence of a holy God.

The Wrath of God

In this regard it is important to say something about
one particular aspect of God's character, namely,
his wrathful hatred of sin. The wrath of God is a
key subject in the Bible. In fact, there are more
references to the wrath or anger of God than there
are to the love of God. To help get a grasp of this,

take time to read through a selection of these: Nahum 1:2-8; Romans 1:18; 2:5-11; 5:9; 12:19; 1 Thessalonians 1:10; 2:16; 5:9; 2 Thessalonians 1:8-10; Revelation 6:16,17 and 16:19.

We must also recognise that there are as many references to God's wrath in the New Testament as there are in the Old Testament. The notion of an angry God in the Old Testament who is replaced by a God of love in the New Testament was a heresy rejected by the early Church and yet is fostered by some today who simply have not studied their Bibles closely enough.

God's wrath is underlined by the evidence of his recorded actions. For example, the period which the Jews spent in Exile (the captivity in Babylon) is described as the result of God's wrath being poured out on a sinful people (2 Chronicles 36:15ff.). We could also look at specific incidents such as the destruction of Sodom and Gomorrah (Genesis 19) or the deaths of Ananias and Sapphira (Acts 5).

The Direction of God's Wrath
The Bible tells us that God's wrath is directed against all who disobey him, who refuse to acknowledge Christ and who continue in sin. For many people, such teaching presents problems. This is for a variety of reasons but principally because they regard anger and wrath as unpleasant and unacceptable, and therefore find it hard to attribute them to God. But God's wrath is an essential characteristic

of his person and nature. It is specifically related to his holiness and to his hatred of sin and evil. Indeed, the Welsh scholar Eryl Davies describes God's wrath as 'the controlled and permanent opposition of God's holy nature to all sin'.[2] This teaching is vital in a day when people do not believe that they are sinners, and do not believe in wrath or judgement.

It has often been rightly said that the preaching of the law of God shows people their sin and prepares them for the gospel which shows them the way of salvation. In a very real sense we can say that men and women will come to Christ for salvation only when they see in all its boldness the biblical teaching about sin and hell and judgement. Yet so often this aspect of Christian belief has been neglected or ignored. No wonder, then, that J.I. Packer talks about the church mumbling about God's love and forgiveness in the face of an evil and materialistic society.

In the middle of the 18th century there was a tremendous revival called the Great Awakening, a movement of the Holy Spirit which affected both Britain and North America. The revival began in earnest in New England when the influential American theologian Jonathan Edwards preached a memorable sermon entitled 'Sinners in the hands of an angry God'.

---

2. Eryl Davies, *An Angry God*, Evangelical Press of Wales, 1991, p. 70.

The Climax of God's Wrath

According to biblical teaching, the climax of the wrath of God is to be a day called the 'Day of wrath' (Romans 2:5), sometimes called the 'Day of Judgement', when God's wrath will be poured out upon those who disobey him and who remain finally impenitent (Revelation 20:7-15 and Matthew 25:31-46). We cannot sufficiently stress the awful and terrible nature of that day. Christian preachers and theologians, as well as poets and hymn writers, have used all the imagery of the Bible (and more) in order to bring home the seriousness of being found on that day without salvation, but words cannot fully describe what awaits those who reject Christ.[3]

Having stressed God's wrath, we must also recognise that this wrath is controlled and that God is long-suffering and patient (2 Peter 3:8-14). It is also a fact that God takes no pleasure in pouring out his wrath on unrepentant sinners (Ezekiel 33:11). The Bible tells us, however, that the time will come when that patience will be at an end and judgement will come.

If we are Christians, then this message ought to act as a spur to evangelism. We must try to reach as many as possible of those who are hardening their hearts against God, warn them of their danger and call them to turn to the Lord Jesus Christ and be saved.

---

3. See John Blanchard, *Whatever Happened to Hell?*, Evangelical Press, 1993.

The people who are in most danger are not the ones we normally think of as hardhearted. The ones who are in the most perilous position are the 'nice people': the good neighbours and good friends, the kindly unbelievers. Most people believe that God will welcome all such into heaven, but the Bible doesn't offer hope for 'nice, kind people' who go through life ignoring God. It is not 'nice' to ignore God. It is not 'good' to turn your back on Jesus Christ. We must make a special effort to tell the nice, kind and outwardly good people that their kindness and goodness will not get them into heaven. The kindest people you know, if they are not believers, are in great danger; the Bible says they are going to hell.

Mistaken views of God
Despite the clear teaching of Scripture, there are many people who have a completely fictional image of God. If they think about God at all they regard him as a rather benevolent uncle, somewhere 'up there', who is very open-minded about things, forgives automatically, and is generally at our beck and call when he is needed. Yet this God, created in their own image, bears no relation at all to the God of the Bible.

Sadly, there are even those within the church who have a wrong view of God and who do not take seriously the fact of sin and God's judgement on it. When these people come across passages in the Bible which suggest that God punishes sin, or is angry with sinners, they simply remove the passages concerned. For example, when we read in 1 Samuel 15 that God told Saul to slaughter the Amalekites, or in Joshua 7 of the destruction of Achan, or the deaths of Ananias and Sapphira in Acts 5, some people tell us that such passages are the result of a very primitive understanding of God. To argue that God was responsible for the deaths of these people, they say, is unreasonable and immoral, and says more about those who wrote the passages than it does about God.

People who hold views like these have simply departed from the historic Christian faith. Instead of submitting to God and his Word they have set themselves over the Word as judges, deciding what we may and may not believe. As a result, there develops a 'Christianity' which is not properly grounded in the Word of God, and fails to give attention to the central issue of sin and the need for forgiveness and new birth.

To be true to the Bible we must emphasise that new birth is necessary both because of the sinful condition of mankind and because of the holy nature of God. These two problems, the sinful condition of our lives and our relationship with a holy God have to be dealt with. Regeneration is the key to the process which leads to the solution of both these problems.

Chapter 3

THE NATURE OF REGENERATION

Having tried to understand why it is that people need to be born again, we must now go further and ask what being born again actually means. At its very simplest, we can say that being born again is what makes a person a Christian. In other words, if you are not born again you are not a Christian.

False Ideas

Many people have false ideas as to what makes a person a Christian. Some believe that anyone who is born in a Christian country is a Christian. Countless thousands of these have never been inside a church (except perhaps at a wedding or a funeral) and have no real interest in Christianity.

Some people believe that anyone who lives a good life is a Christian. I remember reading about a Communist who was being buried and, at the funeral, a friend of his was heard to say, 'He was an atheist and a Communist but he was as good a Christian as you or me'. That friend clearly thought that anyone who tried to live a good life was a Christian, no matter what he or she believed.

Some people believe that anyone who is baptised is a Christian. Indeed, as we shall see presently, the Roman Catholic Church teaches that a child is born again at the moment of baptism. Not only is this view contrary to what the Bible says, but the evidence speaks for itself: thousands of people who have been baptised show no interest in Jesus Christ and no inclination to obey his teaching.

Some people believe that anyone who tries to follow the ethical teaching of the Bible (such as the Ten Commandments) and the teaching of Jesus (such as the Sermon on the Mount) is a Christian. But that is not true either. The Pharisees of Jesus' day kept very strictly to an ethical code but Jesus said that their hearts were not right with God. He made it crystal clear to them (and to us) that outward conformity to rules and regulations is not enough to make a person right with God.

Some people believe that if they have any connection with the church they are Christians. There are those who never attend worship but think that because they give some money to the church or attend a church club or organisation they are automatically Christians. Some people even think that having been involved in the church many years ago is sufficient grounds for claiming to be Christians. I have met people who think that they are Christians because they went to Sunday School when they were children, or because their parents went to church, or because at one time they were in one of the youth organisations of the church.

Some people believe that they are Christians because they have 'joined' the church. But this is to put the cart before the horse! If we are Christians then we ought to join in fellowship with other Christians in a congregation of God's people but the outward act of 'joining' does not make people Christians. Attending a few communicants' classes and then standing up in church with others and taking membership vows does not make someone a Christian. Becoming a Christian is a spiritual matter and has little or nothing to do with having one's name on the membership list of a congregation.

Over against all these different opinions as to what a Christian is, we are now going to look at the Bible and see that a Christian is a person who is born again.

'Rebirth' or 'Regeneration'

The word 'rebirth' or 'regeneration' is found in Titus 3:5. A study of this verse reveals several things.

First of all, given the context in which the word appears (verses 3-7), we can say that rebirth or regeneration was an event in the past which marked a radical break in the lives of those who belonged to the church. Paul (including himself in the description, as we saw earlier) describes what they were like before and after being born again.

The second thing to notice is that this radical change is not the result of anything done by the individual who has experienced it. In case anyone should imagine that being born again is a reward for good behaviour, Paul insists that it is 'not because of righteous things we had done, but because of his mercy' (verse 5). In other words, being born again is something which takes place because of God's love and mercy. We do not deserve it and we cannot earn the right to it. We are totally dependent upon God for it. To be true to the Bible we must insist that the new birth is solely the work of God. Thomas Boston, a minister in the Scottish Borders in the early eighteenth century, explained it with a useful illustration. One person might be born the child of a king, another the child of a beggar, but the child has no hand at all in this difference. Similarly, it is God who decides whether or not a person will be born again.[4]

The third point to be noticed follows on from this. We learn from verse 5 that it is the Holy Spirit who brings about the new birth in the lives of individual men and women. Christians believe that there is one God but that he is 'Three in One': Father, Son and Holy Spirit. It is the work of God the Holy Spirit to bring about new birth.[5]

In a day when the Holy Spirit is the subject of

---

4. *The Complete Works of Thomas Boston*, edited by S. McMillan, William Tegg & Co., 1853, Vol. 8, p.157.
5. There is no space here to explain and defend this notion of God as 'Trinity' but if you are unsure about this and would like to understand it better, read *Shared Life* by Donald Macleod (Christian Focus Publications, 1994).

many books and sermons, it is important to point
out that the primary work of the Holy Spirit is to
take what Jesus did by his life, death and resurrection and apply it to men and women. He has no
independent ministry. His whole preoccupation is
with the continuance and application of the work
of Christ. Supremely, this involves him in our lives
as the one who comes to us and brings about new
birth. In fact, we can say that to be born again is to
be baptised in the Holy Spirit, a subject we shall
come back to shortly.

John 3

Sometimes it is easier to understand theological
words and ideas if we have a practical example.
For this reason, and in order to understand a little
better what it means to be born again, we are going
to consider a story from the Bible.

In John 3 we have the story of an encounter between Jesus and a man called Nicodemus. This
story, more than any other in the whole Bible,
proves that being born again is absolutely vital.
Nicodemus, a Pharisee and a member of the Jewish ruling council, came to Jesus one night and
began to speak to him: 'Rabbi,' he said, 'we know
you are a teacher who has come from God. For no-
one could perform the miraculous signs you are
doing if God were not with him.' How did Jesus
react to this statement? Did he thank him for his
words and welcome him into the kingdom of God?

Did he immediately sign the man on as a disciple? Did he proclaim him to be a Christian? No! Jesus did none of these things. Instead, he interrupted the man in full flight and said, 'I tell you the truth, unless a man is born again, he cannot see the kingdom of God.'

Jesus could not have expressed himself more clearly. He is saying that unless you and I are born again we have no place in God's kingdom. In other words, if we are not born again we are not Christians. Nicodemus was a religious man, but that was not enough. He believed that Jesus had been sent from God, but that was not enough. He believed that what Jesus said was true, but that was not enough. He had to be born again.

Yet there remains great confusion on this matter, even within the church. There are many who tell us that these words do not mean what they say, and others who tell us that this talk about being born again is all right for big time evangelists and mission halls but we must not speak about it in the church! There are even those who would tell us that we must not build a doctrine on this passage because it does not tie in with everything else Jesus said, and is quite different from his normal emphasis. John Murray, a Scottish professor of theology, rightly disagrees: 'It is the logical link between his teaching respecting man's depravity, on the one hand, and his teaching respecting the demands and requirements of the kingdom of God on the other.

The Sermon on the Mount would be unintelligible without the presupposition of the new birth.'[6]

Professor Murray is saying that because we are all sinners it is impossible for us to live according to the Sermon on the Mount. This becomes possible only when we are born again and God the Holy Spirit enables us to live in a new way.

Another frequent misunderstanding about this passage from John 3 concerns verse 5. In that verse we read of being born 'of water and the Spirit', and the confusion arises over the meaning of 'water' in that text. There are mainly two views which are held today. The first teaches *baptismal regeneration*. This position is held by Roman Catholics and some Anglicans, although I have even heard Presbyterian ministers saying something remarkably similar. This school of thought treats baptism as conveying the grace which it signifies, namely regeneration. By this view, if a child is baptised he or she is born again. The other view – sometimes called the *Reformed position* – is that the word 'water' does not refer to baptism at all but to cleansing in the general, spiritual sense. This was certainly the view of John Calvin, the 16th century Reformer. He said, 'By water, therefore, is meant nothing more than the inward purification and invigoration which is produced by the Holy Spirit.'[7]

---

6. *Collected Writings of John Murray*, edited by I. Murray, Banner of Truth, 1977, Vol.2 p.175.
7. Quoted by Murray, p.180.

If 'water' in John 3:5 means baptism, then baptism is essential for salvation. But this would lead to ludicrous conclusions. For example, how can baptism, not at that time even instituted, be essential for the salvation of Nicodemus to whom the comment is addressed? And what of the thief on the cross who was promised by Jesus that he would soon be in Paradise (Luke 23:40-43)? Was he saved as Jesus promised, despite the fact that he did not receive baptism?

The only baptism which is essential for salvation is the baptism with the Holy Spirit, which is another name for the new birth. Given the confused, contradictory and plainly heretical notions floating around today regarding this baptism with the Spirit we need to have a firm grasp of this. Baptism with the Holy Spirit refers to new birth. That is, it concerns the first work of God in the sinner, something which brings him to life and results in all the other changes of which the Bible speaks (look up Matthew 3:11; Mark 1:8; Luke 3:16; John 1:33; Acts 1:5; 11:16 and especially 1 Corinthians 12:13).

Those who argue that the baptism with the Spirit is a second experience coming after new birth, something which is available to all but which not all receive have no biblical warrant for this assertion. Their view contradicts the clear teaching of 1 Corinthians 12:13 which states that 'we were all baptised by one Spirit into one body'. All Christians experience the baptism of the Holy Spirit. It is this baptism of the Spirit which brings us into the body of Christ and into the kingdom of God.

Other Scriptures
Having spent some time thinking about Jesus' words to Nicodemus, we must mention some of the other passages in the Bible which help us to understand the new birth. There are a number of verses which describe Christians as those who are 'born of God'. These are important for confirmation of what we have already seen: John 1:13; 1 John 3:9; 4:7; 5:4; 5:18 and 1 John 2:29. Then there are the passages which describe Christians as those who have been newly created: 2 Corinthians 5:17; Ephesians 2:10 and 4:24.

The Extent of Regeneration
The extent of sin, as we saw in the last chapter, is very great. Because of this it is necessary that the new birth be similarly extensive in its effect on the individual. Stephen Charnock, one of the 17th century English Puritan scholars, underlined this point:

> 'Because there was an universal depravation by the Fall, regeneration must answer it in its extensiveness in every faculty. Otherwise it is not the birth of the man, but of one part only. It is but a new piece, not a new creature. This or that faculty may be said to be new, not the soul, not the man.

We are all over bemired by the puddle of sin, and we must be all over washed by the water of grace.'[8]

Thomas Boston, whom we mentioned earlier, taught that regeneration affected the mind, the will, the affections, the conscience, the memory, the body and the conversation.[9] In other words, it affects everything. Nothing remains the same. That is why Paul said that if anyone is a Christian he is 'a new creation' (2 Corinthians 5:17).

As we come towards the end of this chapter we should add that all of the above might be true in a person's life without that person knowing the time, date and place of this new birth. To be born again is vital, but to be able to say when it happened is less important. It was the well-known 19th century English preacher C.H. Spurgeon who said that a man's ignorance of the time of his birth is no evidence that he is not alive!

Summary

Let us sum up what we have learned so far. We are all sinners and we deserve only the judgement of God. There is nothing that we can do to alter this situation because we are spiritually dead. But God, because of his great love for us, brings his chosen people to life through a miraculous work of his Spirit, called the new birth. Have you been born

8. *The Complete Works of Stephen Charnock*, edited by J. McCosh, James Nichol, 1865, Vol.3 p.27.
9. Thomas Boston, *Works*, Vol. 8, pp.138, 143.

again in that way? If you have not then you are not
a Christian. As Jesus said to Nicodemus, '...no-one
can see the kingdom of God unless he is born again.'

Justification and Sanctification

Two important theological words, 'justification'
and 'sanctification', form the basis of most of the
rest of the book because they describe what happens
after a person is born again. At the end of chapter 2
we saw that there are two problems which need to
be solved before human beings are ready to face
God: our relationship with God needs to be repaired
and our sinful lives need to be changed. Regeneration is the beginning of the solution to both problems, because when we are born again the very first
thing which happens is that God gives us faith (Ephesians 2:8). Faith, in turn, has two results. First, it leads
to pardon and acceptance ('justification') in which
our relationship to God is repaired. Second, it leads
to holiness ('sanctification') in which our new birth
proves itself by the emergence of new life.

We are now going to explore these parallel ac-
tivities of God in the life of the believer. We begin
(in chapters 4-6) by looking at the way in which
new birth leads to *a new relationship with God*.
Then (in chapters 7-12) we shall look at the other
side, the way in which new birth leads to *holiness
of life*. In chapter 13 we shall try to draw the threads
of all this together before discussing (in chapters
14 and 15) how all of this becomes a reality in the
life of an individual.

Chapter 4

RIGHT WITH GOD

We begin by considering what is called the doctrine of *justification by faith*. This doctrine is the answer to the question: 'How can sinners come into the presence of a holy God?'

Put at its simplest, justification by faith means that God declares an individual to be pardoned and accepted on the basis of faith in Jesus Christ.

Romans 3:21-31 is the classic passage for a study of this great biblical doctrine, but we must begin by looking at the argument which Paul is presenting in these early chapters of Romans, so as properly to understand our passage. Romans 1:16-17 could be said to be the text on which the rest of the letter is a commentary. In particular, the statement in verse 17 that a righteousness from God is revealed which is by faith, provides the central affirmation of Paul's theology.

Having stated his position, Paul then demonstrates in 1:18-2:16 that the *Gentiles* (the non-Jews) have failed to achieve righteousness by their own actions. They knew what was right and good but they deliberately ignored this truth and went their own way. On the other hand, the *Jews* (Paul writes about them in 2:17-3:19) were in a privileged position, because they had the Scriptures. God had revealed himself to them in a clear and unmistakeable way. But they too failed to live up to what they knew. They failed to keep the law perfectly. In 3:20 Paul comes to a tragic conclusion: 'Therefore no-one will be declared righteous in his sight by observing the law.' The Gentiles had an innate knowledge of God's law whereas the Jews had it in written form in the Old Testament, but both of them failed to keep it. All, therefore, are guilty in the eyes of God.

Having laid this groundwork Paul then, in 3:21-31, describes God's way of salvation, namely, justification by faith. This was no new teaching. Paul makes that very clear in chapter 4 with reference to Abraham and the point is underlined in Hebrews 11. Faith has always been the way of salvation.

Paul tells us that God the judge is going to grant a free pardon to certain people. But how is this possible? The answer comes in verse 22: 'through faith in Jesus Christ'. Verse 23 then reminds us that 'all have sinned and fall short of the glory of God', underlining the fact that God's gift of a free pardon is completely unmerited and undeserved. Then in verses 24-25 we encounter a number of theological words which, taken together, express what God has done on our behalf. Two of these are 'justification' and 'redemption'.

Justification means to be declared righteous. In

biblical terms we can say that it is an act of God's free grace by which he pardons all our sins and accepts us as righteous in his sight. It is as if God scores our names out of one book and writes them in another. Yet for this to be possible, God's wrath has to be dealt with, and the Bible's central message is that Christ did this when he died on the cross. He turned God's wrath away from us and on to himself, as we shall see more fully in chapter 6.

The other word is 'redemption', which means someone being set free by the payment of a price. If you have ever been unfortunate enough to pawn something you will understand this perfectly! In Paul's day it was used in the slave trade and would refer to someone being bought out of slavery. Today it has the connotation of hostages and kidnap and ransom payments. In biblical terms it means that Christ did something on our behalf and as our substitute. He went to the cross and paid the penalty for sin. In the words of the hymn writer: 'In my place condemned he stood, sealed my pardon with his blood.'

We shall see shortly how Christ achieved this for us, but for the moment we must marvel at this great truth: we can never earn salvation, we must accept it as a free gift from God.

Most people do not understand this. If you were to conduct a survey you would find that most people who believe in heaven also believe that the way to get there is to be good, to love your neighbour,

and to try your best; in other words, to *do* something. But they make the mistake of confusing the
results of salvation with the cause of salvation.

The Bible makes it clear that Christ has done
everything which is necessary for our justification;
he has taken all the steps which are necessary that
we might be right with God. But precisely how did
Christ achieve this for us? How did he make it possible for sinners to come into the presence of a holy
God? To discover the answer to this question we
must go to Hebrews 9 by way of Leviticus 16.

Leviticus 16

In the Old Testament God laid down a form of
worship and service which was based on blood sacrifices. At the heart of this system was the most
important day in the Jewish calendar, the Day of
Atonement. In Leviticus 16 we read about the in-
stitution of the Day of Atonement. Aaron, the
brother of Moses, was the High Priest of Israel and
it was his function, along with all the other priests,
to offer sacrifices to God. The number and the types
of sacrifices were laid down by God. But Aaron
had one duty which was peculiar to himself as High
Priest and which could not be performed by any of
the other priests.

On the Day of Atonement, once each year, on
the tenth day of the seventh month, Aaron was to
enter into the Most Holy Place (sometimes called
the 'Holy of Holies'). This was the inner sanctuary

of the Tent, which was the focal point for worship in Old Testament times until it was replaced by the temple in King Solomon's day. No-one else was ever allowed into this inner room and even the High Priest only went in on this one important day in the year.

While he was in the Most Holy Place the High Priest offered sacrifices to make atonement first for his own sins and then for the sins of the people of Israel. This ritual was to be repeated every year without fail. As we read in Leviticus 16:34: 'This is to be a lasting ordinance for you: Atonement is to be made once a year for all the sins of the Israelites.'

The High Priest was not elected, rather he was chosen and appointed by God from among the people. It was necessary that the High Priest be morally pure and consecrated to the service of God (see Leviticus 21:6 and Psalm 106:16). With that background from Leviticus 16 we now have the key to understanding Hebrews 9.

We have seen in the Old Testament that there was a High Priest who offered sacrifices to God on behalf of the people (particularly that great sacrifice on the Day of Atonement). And so in answer to the question: 'How can sinners come into the presence of a holy God?' the Jews could answer: 'They can come because the High Priest has gone to God on their behalf and has made atonement. Their sins have been passed over and God will not

hold these sins against them'. But when we come
to the New Testament we find something even more
remarkable.

Hebrews 9

Hebrews 9 tells us that Jesus Christ is a High Priest
in a way that no other could ever have been.

(1) The High Priest of the Jews offered the same
sacrifices year after year, but Jesus, with one sacrifice, put an end to all that.

(2) The High Priest in the Old Testament entered into the Most Holy Place to offer the sacrifice of atonement, but Jesus entered into heaven
itself.

(3) The blood of goats and calves did not really
cleanse men and women from sin, it only made
them 'ceremonially' clean; but the blood of Christ
actually cleanses from sin once and for all.

(4) The High Priest in the Old Testament had to
offer sacrifices for his own sins as well as those of
the people, but Jesus was without sin.

By comparing these two chapters of the Bible
we can see that the death of Christ had a much
deeper meaning than we are sometimes given to
imagine. Everything which we read in the Old Testament about sacrifices and priests and so on was
summed up in the cross. The plan of God for the
salvation of his people did not begin when Jesus
was born. Rather the whole Bible stands together
and we can see the fulfilment in Christ of all the

temporary measures instituted in the Old Testament.

An incident recorded in Matthew 27:50-51 helps us to understand the full significance of the High Priesthood of Jesus. At the very moment Jesus died, the curtain in the temple was torn in two. That curtain was the curtain between the outer room and the Most Holy Place. That is to say, it was the curtain which the High Priest passed through going into the Most Holy Place on the Day of Atonement each year. Suddenly, the barrier between the Most Holy Place and the remainder of the temple had been taken away.

Why did this happen? It was a sign from God that the Jewish High Priest was not needed any more. Jesus had fulfilled with one sacrifice everything which was previously done by the High Priest and this had been accepted by God. Any believer can now come into the nearer presence of God at any time, not just one man on one day in the year. And more important still, when we do come into the nearer presence of God we don't come bearing a blood sacrifice; the debt for sin has already been fully paid.

That has implications for our theology and for our practice. The Christian church should speak of 'ministers' or 'pastors', not 'priests'; and we don't need to offer sacrifices, so we have the Lord's Supper around a communion table, not a Mass before an altar.

Put at its simplest, we now have free and unrestricted access into the presence of God. Jesus Christ has made a new and living way for us to come into the presence of God and all the barriers of the Old Testament system have gone (look up Romans 5:1,2; Ephesians 2:18 and 3:12).

But this is not the end of the story. When the Bible tells us that Jesus is our great High Priest and that he is 'the only mediator between God and man' (1 Timothy 2:5-6) it is not only speaking about what he did in the past for us on Calvary, but what he continues to do for us now. The Bible assures us that Jesus, even now, is praying for us before the throne of God (Romans 8:34; Hebrews 7:25 and 1 John 2:1).

A well-known paraphrase of Hebrews 4 puts the whole matter very well:

> Where high the heavenly temple stands,
> The house of God not made with hands,
> A great High Priest our nature wears,
> The Guardian of mankind appears.
>
> He who for men their surety stood,
> And poured on earth his precious blood,
> Pursues in heaven his mighty plan,
> The Saviour and the Friend of man.
>
> With boldness, therefore, at the throne,
> Let us make all our sorrows known;
> And ask the aids of heavenly power,
> To help us in the evil hour.

God, because of his nature, could not ignore sin. It had to be dealt with. So, having declared mankind to be guilty, he passed sentence and then came in the person of his Son and bore that sentence himself on the cross at Calvary.

An illustration of this transaction concerns two friends. During their time at school and as young men they were inseparable, the very best of friends. Gradually, however, over the years, they lost touch with one another. One of them did very well at university and went on to become a judge. The other, unfortunately, fell into bad company and became a criminal. One day the criminal appeared before his friend, now a judge. The judge found his friend guilty as charged but then did something out of the ordinary. He left the bench and went to the office of the clerk of court and paid his friend's fine. He said that, as a friend, he would have liked to declare his friend innocent, but as a judge he was bound to uphold the law and find his friend guilty. The only way out of this dilemma was to pass sentence but then to pay the penalty himself. The fine having been paid the man was free and the law had no more demand upon him.

God was in a similar position with respect to mankind. Because of his justice he was bound to find us guilty of sin, but because of his love he came (in the person of his Son) and paid the penalty himself. This having been done, he is now able to pass the verdict 'justified' rather than the verdict 'condemned'. God's declaration is accepted by faith, yet even the faith which enables us to do this is itself a gift of his grace!

This does not, however, mean that justification is a 'legal fiction' as if God calls people 'just' who are really still sinners. In fact, a wonderful exchange takes place. Jesus takes our sin and we receive his righteousness.

The Reformation

Historically, this great doctrine of justification by faith lay at the very heart of the Protestant Reformation. In 1505 a Roman Catholic monk called Martin Luther entered an Augustinian monastery where he struggled for years to understand God and his grace. He went through many agonies of soul as he tried to find peace and acceptance before God. The story is told that he climbed the steps of St. Peter's in Rome on hands and knees stopping to kiss every step: just one of the ways he tried to earn peace with God.

It was in 1513, when he was studying Romans and Galatians that he came to a proper understanding of justification by faith. He wrote later, 'I felt as if born again, and it seemed to me as though heaven's gates stood full open before me, and that I was joyfully entering therein...' And so the Reformation began, Martin Luther teaching that the doctrine of justification by faith was the article by which the Christian church stands or falls.

The church in our day is much in need of that kind of revival and of a similar recovery of biblical doctrine. J. I. Packer, who has made a particular study of these matters, tells us that the doctrine of justification by faith has been 'the central theme of the preaching in every movement of revival and religious awakening within Protestantism from the Reformation to the present day.'[10]

When we experience the grace of God in justification we too can rejoice, and echo the words of the hymn:

> No condemnation now I dread:
> Jesus, and all in him, is mine!
> Alive in him, my living Head,
> And clothed in righteousness divine.
> Bold I approach the eternal throne,
> And claim the crown through Christ my own.

In each of our lives, justification by faith is the key to a new world. But perhaps there is someone reading this who has not yet been justified by faith in Jesus Christ. Are you absolutely sure that you are not depending upon good works for salvation? You dare not avoid the Bible's teaching that the only way to be right with God, to be pardoned and accepted, is the way of faith: 'Believe in the Lord Jesus Christ and you will be saved' (Acts 16:31).

---

10. J. I. Packer, 'Introductory Essay' to James Buchanan, *The Doctrine of Justification*, Banner of Truth, 1984, p.viii.

The true Christian is the one who can say with the hymn writer:

> My hope is built on nothing less
> Than Jesus' blood and righteousness;
> I dare not trust my sweetest frame,
> But wholly lean on Jesus' Name.
> On Christ the solid rock I stand
> All other ground is sinking sand.

Chapter 5

THE DOCTRINE OF ADOPTION

Introduction

One of the most important doctrines of the Christian faith, and one which is seldom discussed in any detail, is the doctrine of *adoption*. The Bible tells us that when we become Christians God adopts us into his family. When we think of adoption the picture which probably comes to mind is that of an orphaned child being taken into a family. The biblical picture of adoption includes that idea but is much deeper and wider.

In the Bible, adoption is the climax of God's activity in changing an unbeliever into a believer, a sinner into a saint. The process begins with the new birth. When that happens the gift of faith is given. That faith when exercised leads to justification (pardon and acceptance). Then comes adoption.

Taken on its own, justification is a legal concept and might sound cold or remote, but adoption, as the completion of the process, puts that right. It is the great wonder of the Christian gospel that we should not only be forgiven but actually taken into the very family of God.

Professor A.H. Strong, turn of the century American Baptist theologian, puts it like this:

'After serving a term in the penitentiary, the con-
vict goes out with a stigma upon him and with no
friends. His past conviction and disgrace follow
him. He cannot obtain employment. He cannot
vote. Want often leads him to commit crime again;
and then the old conviction is brought up as proof
of bad character, and increases his punishment...
But the justified sinner is differently treated. He
is not only delivered from God's wrath and eternal death, but he is admitted to God's favour and
eternal life. The discovery of this is partly the cause
of the convert's joy. Expecting pardon, at most, he
is met with unmeasured favour. The prodigal finds
the Father's house and heart open to him, and more
done for him than if he had never wandered.'

Bible Passages

There are three passages of Scripture which are
particularly helpful to us as we study this doctrine.
The first of these is Romans 8:12-17. In verse 14
we read that '...those who are led by the Spirit of
God are sons of God'. In other words, only those
who have the Spirit of God in them are the children of God. There is a broad sense in which we
can speak of God as being the Father of everyone
whom he has created, but when the Bible speaks of
the 'children of God' it is normally referring to
believers. There is a myth which is popular today
to the effect that we are all God's children and that
we will all be saved in the end. But this is not what
the Bible teaches. If we have not been adopted into

his family then we do not belong to God and we are not his children. We are not children of God by nature, only by grace. The relationship between God and his children is a relationship effected by a supernatural, sovereign act of grace. It is the presence of the Spirit which enables us to address God as Father. As children of God we are 'heirs' and the inheritance is an eternity in heaven.

The second passage is 1 John 3:1-10, which testifies to the love and grace of God in adoption. Adoption is not something we deserve, it is all of grace. Nevertheless, it is not some last minute idea. Indeed, the Bible tells us that God prepared us for this from all eternity (Ephesians 1:5).

John also makes it clear that humanity is divided into two distinct groups. Thomas Boston put it like this: 'There are but two families in the world, and to one of the two every man and woman belongs. One is Satan's family, the other God's.' Boston also sees the call of the gospel as involving this matter of adoption: 'Our Lord sends his messengers, ministers of the gospel, out into the world among those of Satan's family, to proclaim the offer of adoption unto them, that whosoever of them will leave their father's house and people, shall be adopted into the family of heaven.' [11]

But if we ask the question 'How can we become the children of God?' the answer is found in our third passage, John 1:11-13. Notice in particular

---

11. Thomas Boston, *Works*, Vol.1, p.619.

the phrases, 'to all who received him', 'to all who believed' and, 'he gave the right to become children of God.' Here is the great call of the gospel: believe and you will be saved, and you will be adopted into the family of God.

The *Westminster Confession of Faith*, written in the middle of the seventeenth century and still today a recognised standard of doctrine for Presbyterians all over the world, devotes a chapter to adoption. It is the shortest chapter in the whole *Confession* but one of the most profound:

> 'All those that are justified, God vouchsafeth, in and for his only Son Jesus Christ, to make partakers of the grace of adoption: by which they are taken into the number, and enjoy the liberties and privileges of the children of God; have his name put upon them, receive the Spirit of adoption; have access to the throne of grace with boldness; are enabled to cry, Abba, Father; are pitied, protected, provided for, and chastened by him as by a father; yet never cast off, but sealed to the day of redemption, and inherit the promises, as heirs of everlasting salvation.' [12]

The Great Necessity

The prerequisite for adoption is regeneration. Without that fundamental change there can be no adoption. God only takes into his family those who have

---

12. Chapter 12.

been re-made in his image, who have been transformed by the power of the Holy Spirit into new creatures. In other words, regeneration fits us for adoption by providing us with a new nature and a new disposition.

As the English Puritan Thomas Watson said, 'When a man adopts another for his son and heir, he may put his name upon him, but he cannot put his disposition into him; if he be of a morose rugged nature, he cannot alter it; but whom God adopts he sanctifies; he not only gives a new name but a new nature. 2 Peter 1:4.'[13] In one sense we can say that we are re-born into the family of God (John 1:12), but in a real sense adoption comes later, and regeneration is simply the preparation for that greater gift.

People today need to feel a sense of belonging and to have a sense of purpose about life. This doctrine is not some arid theological term but an expression of a tremendous reality.

---

13. Thomas Watson, *A Body of Divinity*, Banner of Truth, 1983, p.233.

Chapter 6

THE ATONEMENT

In our chapter on justification we emphasised the work of Jesus Christ in securing salvation. We must now pause to underline the crucial importance of what Christ has done for those who trust in him.

The story of Jesus' death and resurrection is well known but I sometimes wonder if we really understand what it means. The best way to establish whether or not we understand it is to present the issue in the form of a question: 'How can the death and resurrection of one man 2,000 years ago affect me today?'

The Lamb of God

In order to answer this question let us look at some words of John the Baptist when he introduced Jesus by saying, 'Look, the Lamb of God, who takes away the sin of the world!' (John 1:29). It might seem strange to take an incident right at the beginning of Jesus' ministry in order to explain the meaning of his death and resurrection, but these words take us to the very heart of the significance of the cross.

The first thing we must establish is why John

used this strange expression. If we today were to describe someone as a 'lamb' it might be that we considered the person to be gentle or kind. But that is not what was in the mind of John the Baptist. As a Jew, he was using language which would immediately have been understood by those who were listening to him. He was making reference to the Passover lamb, an important Old Testament concept that we can begin to understand by going back in Jewish history to the time of Joseph, the son of Jacob.

Joseph had been sold into slavery by his brothers but, by a series of amazing circumstances, he eventually found himself in an entirely unexpected position, as a leader in Egypt, second only to Pharaoh himself. He used this position wisely and well to safeguard the country from disaster during years of famine. As a reward, he and his family were given good land in Egypt and they settled there. In due course, however, a new Pharaoh came to power who did not know his country's history, and did not know about Joseph. He and his people began to be suspicious of the Hebrews (as Joseph's people were called) and were concerned lest they join with the enemies of Egypt in the event of a war.

As a result, they made the Hebrews into slaves and ill-treated them. The Hebrews cried out to God for deliverance and, hearing their cries, God sent Moses to liberate them. Pharaoh was unwilling to let them go and unwilling to listen to Moses or to be persuaded by the miracles which Moses performed. Because of this, God brought many judgements upon the Egyptians. Finally, Moses told Pharaoh that God was going to bring one last plague upon Egypt: the firstborn son of every Egyptian family was going to die.

Moses told all the Hebrews to prepare themselves for the night when this would happen. They were to take a lamb, kill it and put some of its blood on the sides and tops of the doorframes of their houses (Exodus 12:7). When God came to Egypt in judgement he would see the blood and would 'pass over' the houses which were marked by the blood of the lamb.

This awful night duly came round and everything happened as God had said it would. And since that time – even to the present day – the Jews have remembered the Passover as the night when they were liberated from oppression in Egypt and when they sheltered under the blood of the lamb.

Explanation

If we now go back to the words of John the Baptist we can begin to understand what he meant when he called Jesus the Lamb of God who takes away the sin of the world. Just as the Israelites in Egypt took shelter under the blood of the lamb and so escaped when God came to Egypt in judgement, so we are to take shelter under the blood of Jesus Christ to escape from God's wrath and judgement today.

This interpretation of the words of John the Baptist is supported elsewhere in the Bible. Paul, in 1 Corinthians 5:7 says that 'Christ, our Passover Lamb, has been sacrificed'. In Isaiah 53:7 the Messiah is described as being 'led like a lamb to the slaughter'. In Revelation 5:6,9,12 Jesus is described as 'the Lamb who was slain' and it is said that with his 'blood' (verse 9) he purchased men for God.

If we now draw the threads of all this together we can go some way towards answering the question with which we began. We are all sinners in need of salvation. God has provided this salvation. Just as he provided a way in Egypt for the Israelites to escape from death on that terrible night, so he has provided a way for us to escape the judgement of God on that terrible day when he will judge the world. Just as the Jews in Egypt were safe because they sheltered under the blood of a lamb sprinkled on the doorframes of their houses, so today we are safe if we shelter under the blood of Christ. When Jesus died on the cross at Calvary he did so as a sacrificial offering for sin. God chose to accept the death of Christ in our place. He punished Jesus instead of punishing us. Christ is our Passover lamb and his blood has been shed for all who will come to him by faith.

It is important, however, to stress that Jesus of Nazareth was a real man with a real humanity. What he did on the cross he did *for* us and *as one of* us. In the history of the Christian Church there have always been those who denied either the divinity of Jesus Christ or his humanity. In the early Church some denied his humanity, saying that he was a god only pretending to be a man. In our day there are theologians who deny his divinity, arguing that the idea of a god becoming a human being is unbelievable and mythological. In its creeds and confessions, the Christian Church has always resisted the pressure from both sides, insisting that Jesus of Nazareth was indeed both God and man at the same time, by virtue of the Incarnation and by means of two natures in one person. But why have people argued over this? Is it really important?

The Humanity of Jesus

Jesus of Nazareth was born in the normal way to a human mother. Bruce Milne, the contemporary Scottish theologian, puts it like this: 'He was a developing foetus in the womb of Mary and came into the world through a human birth canal at the climax of a normal period of gestation and labour'.[14] That is the clear implication of Matthew 1:18-25 and of other passages of Scripture.

There is a good deal of other evidence in the New Testament which underlines the humanity of Jesus. There were times when he experienced hunger and thirst, when he was tired and weary, when

14. Bruce Milne, *Know the Truth*, IVP, 1982, p.125.

he was angry or sad and so on. This is to say nothing of the very fact that he could bleed and die.

Perhaps the greatest passage of all in relation to the humanity of Christ is Philippians 2:6-8. Speaking of Jesus Christ, Paul writes, 'Who, being in very nature God, did not consider equality with God something to be grasped, but made himself nothing, taking the very nature of a servant, being made in human likeness. And being found in appearance as a man, he humbled himself and became obedient to death – even death on a cross.'

But why was it so important that God should come to this earth as a man? The answer is that the second person of the Trinity came to this earth as a man in order to die and so bring salvation to all who would put their faith in him. In order to understand how this was accomplished we must return to the early chapters of the Book of Genesis and then compare what we find there with Romans 5 and 1 Corinthians 15.

When the first man, Adam, was created he stood in perfect moral and spiritual equilibrium. In other words, he had free will and was able to choose between good and evil: to obey God or disobey God. He was perfect yet capable of losing that perfection. There was nothing in all creation (except Satan) which could possibly have inclined him to evil. God had done everything for his good. But yet he chose to disobey God and the Fall took place (Genesis 3).

When Adam sinned and broke his covenant with God, the result of that disobedience brought sin and judgement upon every human being because Adam stood before God not simply as a private individual but also as the representative of the whole human race. Since then, mankind has had a natural tendency towards sin and evil and every person born is a sinner. We don't need to believe the Bible to see the truth of this statement, we need only take notice of what is happening in the world around us.

What then should God do? Abandon the human race? Destroy it and begin again? God chose another way. He decided to send a second representative man, someone who would succeed where Adam had failed, someone who would obey where Adam had disobeyed. This is the great truth expressed in Romans 5:18. Speaking of Adam and Christ, Paul writes, 'Consequently, just as the result of one trespass was condemnation for all men, so also the result of one act of righteousness was justification that brings life for all men. For just as through the disobedience of the one man the many were made sinners, so also through the obedience of the one man the many will be made righteous.'

In 1 Corinthians 15:21,22 Paul underlines this point: 'For since death came through a man, the resurrection of the dead comes also through a man. For as in Adam all die, so in Christ all will be made alive.'

Where Adam disobeyed, Christ obeyed; where Adam failed, Christ succeeded. And so we have a new Head, a new covenant, a second chance. As the hymn writer says,

> O loving wisdom of our God
> when all was sin and shame,
> A second Adam to the fight
> And to the rescue came.
>
> O wisest love! that flesh and blood
> which did in Adam fail,
> should strive afresh against the foe,
> should strive and should prevail.

How wonderful that God should do all this for us! But even this was not all. In addition, this 'second man' gave himself as a sacrificial offering, received in his own person God's judgement upon sin, and so brought forgiveness and salvation to all who would come to him in faith.

Perhaps now we can see why the humanity of Jesus is so important and why it was necessary for God the Son to become a man. John Calvin put it like this:

'... our Lord came forth as true man and took the person and the name of Adam in order to take Adam's place in obeying the father, to present our flesh as the price of satisfaction to God's righteous judgement, and, in the same flesh, to pay the

penalty that we had deserved. In short, since neither as God alone could he feel death, nor as man
alone could he overcome it, he coupled human
nature with divine...' [15]

It is a matter of history that Jesus of Nazareth
was taken to the cross at Calvary, was crucified,
and died. It is important to understand something
of the theology of the cross if we are to make sense
of that story. In particular, we must understand that
God chose to become a man in order to bring salvation to a lost world. He did so in the person of
Jesus of Nazareth who was, and ever remains, both
God and man at the same time. The real humanity
of Jesus was crucial to the accomplishing of this
great mission because what Jesus did on the cross
he did for us. Therefore he had to be one of us and
one with us, a truth expressed in the hymn writer's
words:

> In my place condemned he stood
> sealed my pardon with his blood.

Justification and adoption are only possible,
then, because of what Jesus Christ has done for us.
We can be pardoned, accepted and adopted into
God's family because he has paid the price, he has
taken our punishment.

---

15. John Calvin, *Institutes of the Christian Religion*, edited by J.T. McNeill, Westminster Press, 1977, Vol. 1, p.
466 (section 2/12/3).

Chapter 7

CHRISTIAN HOLINESS

We now come to deal with the other strand of God's work in the life of the believer, namely, sanctification or Christian holiness. The importance of this theme can be stated as follows:

It can be demonstrated from Scripture that, from beginning to end, the purpose of God has been to create a holy people for himself with whom he can have fellowship.

Given the state of our world today, and indeed given the state of the Church, the overwhelming need of our day and generation is for an emphasis on practical Christian holiness.

There are few subjects which are as important for our own spiritual growth and the development of our Christian lives as the study of Christian holiness.

In order to understand what holiness is and why it is important we must consider a very important statement in 1 Peter 1:15-16. These are key verses for a study of Christian holiness. Peter tells his readers to be holy because God is holy, and he supports this with a quotation from Leviticus 11:44, 45 which says the same thing. The phrase 'Be holy, because I am holy' tells us a great deal about God, about ourselves, and about the way we are to live. Let's break it down a little: What does the word 'holy' mean? In what sense is God holy?

1. What Does The Word 'Holy' Mean?

It is difficult to be precise about the exact meaning of the words, both in the Hebrew Old Testament and in the Greek New Testament, which are translated as 'holy' in our English Bibles. It would seem, however, that the root meaning is 'separation' or 'cleansing' or 'purity' or 'consecration'. These Hebrew and Greek words occur about 1,300 times in the Bible, thus demonstrating their importance.

In the Bible, the word 'holy' is a religious word. It is not a word which is found or used except in the context of the religious life of the people. That is to say, it is not a word which was in everyday use and was taken up and given a religious dimension, as was the case with 'justification'. It is purely a religious word. Early in the Old Testament it is most often used to describe aspects of religious ritual and ceremony (such as when it is used of the cleansing of the priests' garments). In other words, it is used to describe those things which are set apart for God and for his worship. As Professor R.A. Finlayson of the Free Church of Scotland has written: 'In the Old Testament holiness is designated of places, things, seasons, and official persons, in virtue of their connection with the worship of God... holiness signifies a relation that involved separation from common use and dedication to a sacred one.'[16] There are a number of references which help to underline this point, including Exodus 3:5; 8:28; 16:23; 28:2; 29:6; 30:25 and Leviticus 8:9.

As the Old Testament goes on, but more especially in the New Testament, the word 'holy' takes on a moral and ethical dimension. It no longer refers simply to the ritual and ceremonial aspects of religious life but refers to character and behaviour. And so we can speak of the holiness of an individual, and the holiness (or otherwise) of a particular course of action (Ephesians 1:4; 1 Peter 1:15).

2. In What Sense Is God Holy?

Having said something about what holiness is and what it means, we must now say that, supremely, the word is used to describe God. It is used to describe God in two ways. First, it describes what God is like, in and of himself. That is to say, it tells us that the essential characteristic of God is holiness. This is most important. The Bible tells us many things about God but it clearly teaches that when everything else is stripped away holiness is what characterises God. J.I. Packer has said that holiness '...means, quite comprehensively, the God-ness of God, everything about him which sets him apart from man'[17] (cf. Isaiah 6:3; 40:25).

---

16. R.A. Finlayson, 'Holiness' in *New Bible Dictionary*, IVP, 1962.
17. J. I Packer, *God's Words*, IVP, 1981, p.171.

This is very important and must be stressed. Many people today, even professing Christians, worship a false god, because they do not worship this holy God who is revealed to us in the Bible. I think it would be true to say that the great emphasis today is on a God whose primary characteristic is love. Those who insist on this emphasis, as we saw in chapter 2, then set God's love over against his judgement, as if these things were incompatible. Hence many do not believe in hell because the god they worship is so characterised by love that he could not and would not send anyone to hell. Only when we understand that the primary characteristic of God is holiness (with both love and judgement included in that general heading) can we attain any kind of balanced doctrine of the nature of God. Many biblical statements confirm this including, for example, Leviticus 11:44,45; 19:2; 20:26; 21:8 and Revelation 4:8.

The second way in which holiness is used to describe God concerns his actions. The Bible makes it clear to us that God is not only holy in and of himself but holy in his relations with, and his actions towards, his creatures. We can see this, for example, in Psalm 145:17 which reads: 'The LORD is righteous in all his ways and loving towards all he has made'.

We Are To Be Holy

God's command 'Be holy' has an obvious and important implication, namely, that we are not holy already. This may be too obvious to say, but let us simply rehearse in our minds the facts of the case. As we saw in the last chapter, when Adam fell he brought upon himself and also upon his posterity (including us) the consequences of that Fall, namely, sin and judgement. Hence every single person who has ever been born (except Christ) has suffered the consequences. Thus we are all born as sinners. This transfer of sin and guilt from the one theologians call our 'federal representative' to us is called 'imputation'. Before we do anything good or bad we stand under the curse and judgement of God as objects of his wrath. We compound the seriousness of the situation by actual sins, which demonstrate the true condition of our nature. By our birth into a fallen race and by our sinful behaviour we show ourselves to be children of our father, the devil, until we are rescued from that condition by God.

These doctrines of the Fall, sin, imputation of sin and so on are summarised by what is sometimes called 'total depravity'. This does not mean that we are as bad as we could be (we have God's common grace to thank for that) but that every aspect and area of our life is affected and damaged by sin. Indeed, although we are made in the image of God, that image within us is so defaced and corrupted as to require the work of the Holy Spirit to restore it.

The Bible's clear teaching on this can be easily confirmed. We live in a world where human life is cheap, where abortion is commonplace, where violence, torture, murder, rape, abduction and all manner of evil is rampant and on the increase. Hardly a day goes past without some appalling tragedy being brought to our attention by the mass media. If it is not children caught in the crossfire of a war, it is mindless violence or political terrorism.

Yet some people speak of a 'civilised world'. It seems hard to believe now that immediately before World War I the great hope was of continual progress towards utopia, and people (including theologians) painted a picture of a world which would gradually benefit from modern science and technology, and from which all evil would disappear as men and women shared with one another the good fruits of the technological revolution. Uninterrupted progress was the hope of the day – until that hope was shattered by two World Wars within a generation, and by the horrors of Auschwitz and Belsen, and the systematic mass murder of six million Jews.

Why was that optimism destined to come to nothing? Why was the future vision of perpetual progress completely and utterly destroyed? Because the creators of the vision, the architects of the new world, failed to take into their consideration the most vital element in the whole puzzle – human sin.

Theologians began to speak of sin as if it had to do with systems and not hearts, as if there were no sinners, merely unwilling victims of sinful circumstances. They denied that there was a devil, spoke of the innocence of mankind and refused to believe that every person born on this planet (except Christ) is a sinner who is cut off from God because of that sin. They believed that if they changed people's circumstances they would change the people. Then they found that man was incapable of living at peace with his neighbour because he was not at peace with God.

Their unbiblical theology, which was sometimes called the 'social gospel', crumbled and died in the face of appalling evil such as the world had never seen, even in the darkest days of the sadistic Roman Emperor Nero.

You cannot construct a biblical theology without taking sin into account. It is the central factor. It is that which caused the fall from perfection and estranges us from God. It is what put Christ on the cross and explains all the wickedness and criminality of our day and generation. There can be no rational explanation of the way things are without a coherent doctrine of sin.

The problem is such that, even after the death of the social gospel, some within the church still refuse to take sin seriously. As a result, people question whether the church is standing up for biblical standards. Is the church declaring the need for men and women to be born again of the Holy Spirit and to seek to live godly lives, lives of holiness? Sadly, we have to say that it does not always do so. Standards of morality which would previously have been taken for granted are now being challenged. For example, homosexuality is increasingly being regarded by many as a valid alternative lifestyle to heterosexuality. It is now almost commonplace to hear senior figures within the churches say that the church should give its blessing to stable homosexual and lesbian relationships, and so on. Where is the biblical teaching on holiness in all of this?

Those within the church who take this kind of line are retreating in the face of the world, and are now beginning to sanction behaviour and standards which are entirely contrary to what we find in Scripture. The consensus of opinion within society rather than the authority of God's inspired Word becomes the determining factor in decision-making. If a majority of people come to accept something as legitimate then the church often follows meekly on. Instead of being a light shining in the darkness, the world is told that its darkness is simply a new kind of light.

How Can We Be Holy?

Over against all this, Peter tells us to be holy because God is holy. But how can this be? Given that every person born on this planet is a sinner, given the state of our world, given the often pathetic weakness of the church in the face of the consensus in society, how can we be holy? The answer lies in the fact that God did not give us up. Even in our depravity he desired to save out of the mass of fallen humanity some with whom he could have fellowship, by making them holy.

The Old Testament sacrificial system describes some 'temporary measures' taken by God as a preliminary step towards the day when Jesus Christ, the second Person of the Trinity, would be born, live, die and rise again in order to cleanse his people from sin and create a holy people for his Father. This theme of holiness is so much at the centre of everything which God has done since the beginning that it would be possible to write a whole systematic theology, dealing with all the major doctrines of grace, with holiness as the connecting theme.

But to return to our question: how can we become holy? The answer is simple yet profound. We can become holy only through the action of God the Father in choosing us, the work of Jesus Christ on the cross in dying for us, and the work of the Holy Spirit in applying to us what Christ has accomplished on our behalf.

In this chapter we have focused on the holiness of God and on his demand that his people be holy too. In the next chapter we go on to consider the relationship between the new birth and Christian holiness.

Chapter 8

CHANGED LIVES

We must now consider the results of new birth. In other words, what practical difference does it make? Are people who are born again different? If so, how can we recognise them?

The Bible teaches that new birth leads to new life. It even goes so far as to say that if someone who claims to have become a Christian does not show evidence of new life, then we must conclude that there has been no new birth.

Let us begin to examine this teaching by considering Titus 2:1-3:8. In doing so we shall see that doctrine (what we believe) is immensely practical! (This is probably a much-needed element at this stage in our study when there has been a great deal of doctrine and not too much practical application.)

For Paul, doctrine always has practical implications, it always leads to action. In other words, what you believe always has implications for the way you live. This means that Christian doctrine is not simply an academic subject for scholars. Rather, it should be the interest and concern of every Christian. Doctrine is simply a structured presentation of what we believe. Unfortunately, some people have an interest in doctrine which is not practical. This is dangerous. Sound doctrine is not meant to be a kind of talisman to prove our orthodoxy, rather it is meant to help us live. A good test would be this: if your doctrine leads you to live a better Christian life then it is good doctrine, but if it does not then it is worthless. Having said that, however, we must stress that doctrine is important. Almost all sinful practices can be traced to a mistake in what people believe. Right believing should lead to right living. The two belong together.

In Titus 2:11-14 Paul says that the salvation which comes by the grace of God ought to have certain results in the life of the believer. In particular it enables the newly born Christian '...to say "No" to ungodliness and worldly passions, and to live self-controlled, upright and godly lives...' (verse 12). Paul then goes even further and says that the whole purpose of Jesus Christ in dying upon the cross was '...to purify for himself a people that are his very own, eager to do what is good' (verse 14). This is very important. In the beginning, when God created our first parents, Adam and Eve, they were holy and without sin. As we have seen, that changed with the entrance of sin and disobedience into the world as recorded in Genesis 3. Ever since then, God's plan has been to restore that situation, to create once again a people who would live holy lives in obedience to his will. The new birth is the key to the whole operation. But it is not an end in itself.

Its purpose is to enable people to live holy lives.

Paul's letter to Titus, then, shows that the new birth has only truly taken place where we see the development of purity and holiness. In short, if there is no new life, there has been no new birth. If we read on into chapter 3 we see this point underlined. In verse 3 Paul describes what he and the other Christians were like before God met them and changed them. Then, he explains how the change came about:

> 'But when the kindness and love of our Saviour appeared, he saved us, not because of righteous things we had done, but because of his mercy. He saved us through the washing of rebirth and renewal by the Holy Spirit, whom he poured out on us generously through Jesus Christ our Saviour...' (verses 4-6).

What was it that caused the change? It was the 'rebirth' brought about by the Spirit of God. Do you see the point of all this? Spiritual rebirth is not some out-of-the-body experience, nor is it an intellectual voyage of discovery. It is quite simply an act of God whereby he changes the life of an individual so that holiness and purity replace sin and disobedience.

Faith and Action

In the Bible there is one passage which perhaps more than any other underlines the necessary connection between new birth and new life: James 2:14-26. This passage is, I believe, one of the most crucial passages for a proper understanding of the New Testament. It concerns the relationship between faith and action.

If you were to go out on to the streets of any major city in the United Kingdom and ask people if they think that they will go to heaven when they die, a majority would probably still say 'yes'. But if you were to go on to ask the basis for that confidence you would find two different answers.

On the one hand you would get those who say, 'I've always tried to live a good life. I do my best to help people. I've never deliberately hurt anyone. I go to church regularly', or some such answer. These people believe that salvation is by works. On the other hand you would get those who say that they are saved by believing, by trusting in Jesus. These people believe that salvation is by faith. One group believes that salvation has to do with action, the other believes that it has to do with faith.

Yet even within the Christian church there is confusion concerning the relationship between faith and action. For many, there is a major problem in what seems at first glance to be a contradiction in the Bible between what James says and what Paul says at Romans 4:1-3. One has only to read Paul's words to see why people suggest he is at odds with James, but this is not the case. How can these views be reconciled?

The answer to the apparent problem lies in properly understanding the relation between what you believe and what you do, between faith and action. Putting it at its simplest, Paul is teaching us very properly that salvation is by faith, but James is teaching us that true faith shows itself in practical action. This connection between faith and works is directly related to the connection between the doctrines of justification and sanctification. This connection is the key, not only to understanding James 2, but also the key to understanding Christianity. In other words, when someone is justified by faith that new relationship with God leads to a changed life.

It is important that we do not misunderstand what is being said here. God does not say, 'You have become a Christian, therefore be good'. Rather he says, 'If you have become a Christian you will be good.' It is vital that we understand this connection. With this in mind, let's now consider James' words in more detail. In this passage James is dealing with someone who is claiming to be a Christian when there is no evidence to support the claim. Essentially, James tells us that such a situation is unthinkable. If Christ has entered a person's life then there will be results. James was prepared to accept a person's profession of faith only if it resulted in godly living.

Words are not enough (verse 16). Doctrine is not enough (verse 19). I well remember Professor Sinclair Ferguson saying that a man could have the most exalted theology and yet still have the heart and mind of a natural man. In other words, you can believe all the right things and yet still be an unconverted sinner.

As Christians we tend to judge people by their doctrine. Are they 'sound'? Do they believe the right things? Some Christians can sniff out a heresy at twenty paces but the Bible tells us that the primary test of Christian faith is Christian action. Please do not misunderstand me. I would be the very last person to play down the importance and significance of sound Christian doctrine. What we believe is vital. But doctrine is not the only test, indeed it is not the fundamental test. There are many soundly-converted people whose doctrinal understanding is confused and mistaken and who believe all kinds of wrong things. That situation can be sorted out given the right teaching and a thirst for the Scriptures.

Christian living is the fundamental test. If the root of the matter is in us at all then we will give evidence of that by our works. New life is the primary evidence of new birth. In verse 18 James makes the position clear: the only way of demonstrating or proving that we have faith is by our lives.

In the rest of the passage, James illustrates this truth by using two examples, Abraham and Rahab.

Both were saved by what can be called 'faith-works'. That is to say, their faith in God resulted in certain action and so they pleased God.

In the closing verse of the chapter (verse 26) James repeats what he has already said in verse 17: 'faith without deeds is dead'. The basic claim of this passage is that if Christ has truly entered a person's life then there will be results. It is also important to stress the outward, verifiable, nature of this change. James is not saying that we must prove to ourselves that the change has taken place. As sinners we shall always be easily persuaded that we are better than we really are! Instead, James is saying that the change which takes place when someone is reborn is a change which will be obvious to others.

In Romans 6:1-14 we see further evidence of the relationship between new birth and new life. Here, Paul is at pains to point out that the new Christian has died to sin and must live in it no longer.

Some time ago I was listening to a preacher who was speaking about the change required in becoming a Christian. Many people, he said, reject Christianity because they recognise that their lives will have to change, but they see the change in purely negative terms. They will have to give up this or that, refrain from doing this or that and generally stop enjoying themselves! What they don't realise, said the preacher, is that the change required is not some painful hair-shirt approach but a glorious liberation. He used the illustration of an old tub which his family kept in the garden. It was full of tadpoles but there came a time when the tadpoles became frogs and left the tub. This was not a painful experience for them at all, rather it would have been painful for them to have stayed where they were. They were no longer content with the old environment, it could no longer satisfy them. They needed to exercise their new found freedom in a more appropriate environment.

That is precisely what Paul is saying here. If you have become a Christian, you have been set free, you have died to sin, died to self, therefore do not look back! The new life which we begin when we are born again is not full of misery but full of joy, not full of regret that we can no longer live as we used to live, but full of regret that we ever lived that way in the first place!

Sanctification: Definitive and Progressive
The transformation which begins to take place when we are born again is called sanctification ('being made holy'). Becoming more holy (in other words, more like Jesus) is generally a long, slow process and the Holy Spirit is working in us from the moment we are born again until the moment we die in order to take us on that long journey. This process will never be finished, because we shall never be perfectly holy in this life, never completely without sin.

The first thing to be said, then, is that becoming holy is a process, not an instantaneous act of God. Yet this is not the whole story, because something of the work of making us holy is accomplished by the Spirit of God as soon as we are born again. The theologians have used different words to describe this but more recently, among evangelical theologians, it has been called *definitive sanctification*.

We can see this in various parts of the Bible. For example, in 1 Corinthians 1:2 Paul describes those to whom he is writing as 'those sanctified in Christ Jesus and called to be holy'. Notice what is being said here. On the one hand these Corinthian Christians are described as 'sanctified', which would suggest that they are already holy, but on the other hand they are 'called to be holy', which suggests that they are not yet holy. How is this to be resolved? The answer is that some of the work of making them holy was done instantaneously when they were born again, but the remainder would be accomplished more slowly, by means of an ongoing process.

The holiness which the Holy Spirit immediately effects in the believer at the moment of spiritual rebirth is what is being referred to when we speak of definitive sanctification. I well remember Captain Stephen Anderson saying that before becoming a Christian he used to swear regularly. It was some weeks after being born again that he noticed that he had not sworn at all. He did not say, 'Well,

I have become a Christian, now I must give up swearing', it simply disappeared. That was the work of the Holy Spirit in definitive sanctification. Many other biblical references could be studied on this point, including 1 Corinthians 6:11; 2 Timothy 2:21; Acts 15:9; 1 Peter 2:24 and 1 John 3:6-9.

The other aspect of the work of sanctification in the life of the Christian is called *progressive sanctification*. This is the work of the Holy Spirit by which, over many years, an individual is gradually changed into the likeness of Jesus Christ and becomes more holy and more righteous. This process can be long and painful. I have just given one example from the life of Stephen Anderson but Stephen would readily admit that, whereas his swearing disappeared suddenly and without effort, there were other battles to be won against sin and disobedience which took longer and were more painful and more costly. There can be many sins, and many patterns of ingrained sinful behaviour which require to be broken and changed, and are only dealt with over a long period.

Paul understood this perfectly and in Romans 7:15-25 he opens his heart in an honest statement of this truth, particularly in verse 19: 'For what I do is not the good I want to do; no, the evil I do not want to do – this I keep on doing.' Surely all of us who are Christians could testify to that experience? Progressive sanctification is a process of change in which there must be honesty and admission of

guilt and failure. John says: 'If we claim to be without sin we deceive ourselves and the truth is not in
us. If we confess our sins, he is faithful and just
and will forgive us our sins and purify us from all
unrighteousness' (1 John 1:8,9).

In other words, we must recognise that we are
sinners who are in the process of becoming holy.
We get a good start because of the definitive sanctification which the Holy Spirit effects in us when
we are born again, but the remainder of that work
goes on slowly and painfully until we go to heaven
to be with God. If we begin to have a high opinion
of ourselves or (God forbid) even imagine that we
have 'arrived' and are completely sanctified, then
we have failed to understand what the Bible is saying.

On the other hand, we must not use the fact that
sanctification is a long process as an excuse for
continuing in sin! If we claim to be Christians, born
again of the Holy Spirit, then the sanctifying work
of the Holy Spirit will be obvious in our lives. We
could simplify all this by saying that the work of
the Holy Spirit in the life of the Christian is to bring
about a change so that the child of God reflects the
nature of the heavenly Father. Thomas Boston put
it like this:

'The moral perfections of the divine nature are, in
measure and degree, communicated to the renewed
soul: thus the divine image is restored; so that, as

the child resembles the father, the new creature resembles God himself, being holy as he is holy.'[18]

In this chapter we have been concerned with this great truth, that new birth leads to new life, and that this new life is a holy life. There are many other passages in the Bible which help to underline this. Think, for example, of the many places where trees and fruit are used to explain Christian life. When Jesus said that a bad tree could not produce good fruit and that a good tree could not produce bad fruit (Matthew 7:18, compare 3:10) he was really saying that new birth leads to new life. When Paul described the fruit of the Spirit in Galatians 5 he was spelling out what the life of a newly-born Christian should be like. We ought also to say that the results of new birth as seen in a holy and sanctified life are not simply for this life. They are a means of preparing us for heaven. As he makes us holy, the Spirit is preparing us to live for ever in the presence of a holy God.

Evidence and Assurance

We began by asking some questions: 'What difference does new birth make? Are people who are born again different? If so, how can we recognise them?' If we take these together, we find that there is really only one question: How can I recognise a true Christian?

---

18. Thomas Boston, *Works*, Vol.8, p.158.

There are many ways in which we could try to answer this question. For example, we could use the words of Jesus: 'All men will know that you are my disciples if you love one another' (John 13:35). Undoubtedly, love is an evidence of real Christianity. If we go through the Bible carefully we shall discover that there should also be a love for God's Word (the Bible) and a desire to pray. There should be a concern for evangelism. There should also be a concern for truth and 'sound doctrine'.

Above all, however, the evidence that someone is a Christian is the evidence of a changed life. In the last analysis, holiness is what proves new birth. Unfortunately, some people look for evidence and assurance in places other than the changed life of the believer. In the Bible readings he gave at the 1987 Keswick Convention, the British preacher David Jackman made two points which are relevant to this subject:

> The false apostles in Corinth made great claims about their spiritual experiences and achievements but there were no signs of Christian character.

> It follows that we must be suspicious of meetings where claims are made that this is the greatest thing that has happened since the Day of Pentecost. That's not proof. The proof is in changed lives and character. The proof of new birth is character and holiness, not miracles.

A word of caution as we bring this chapter to a close. All this talk of holiness and sanctification as being the evidence that someone is really a Christian might lead to despair. In my own life as I consider my sin and how little apparent progress has been made in dealing with sin, I could easily come to the conclusion that I am not a Christian at all. That would be wrong. The devil is always trying to bring us down, and we must fight against him. Although, to my shame, there is much sin in my life which ought to have been dealt with many years ago, yet still I trust in God. There is much work still to be done, but the very fact that it has started at all is evidence of God's grace.

Even the most holy of Christians (who put the rest of us to shame) find that the deeper the work of God's Spirit in their lives the more obvious is their sin. John Calvin said that it is only when we turn from contemplating God in all his glory and then turn to consider our own lives that we see how utterly sinful we are.[19] The problem is that most of us compare ourselves to other human beings and so have a 'guid conceit of ourselves'.

Tom Swanston, a Church of Scotland minister in Inverness and a spiritual giant, said to a fellow minister a short time before he died that he could see little evidence of sanctification in his life. And yet everyone else could see it! Tom was such a man of God and so conscious of God's holiness that he

19. John Calvin, *Institutes*, Vol. 1 p.37 (section 1/1/2).

thought himself inadequate and unsanctified. He was so close to the Light of the world that the re-flected light to be seen in his own life seemed to him very dim. To those of us who were further away it was radiant.

Having made that cautionary point we finish on the more positive note that it is good to reflect on one's sanctification because it provides assurance that we have been truly born again, and gives us cause to worship God for his goodness and grace. In Thomas Boston's words: '...the neglect of self-examination leaves most men under sad delusions as to their state, and deprives many saints of the comfortable sight of the grace of God in them.' [20]

---

20. Thomas Boston, *Works*, Vol.8, p.162.

Chapter 9

MORTIFICATION

So far we have concentrated on God's work in us whereby he both initially and progressively makes us holy. Now we look at the other side of the coin, namely, the action which *we* have to take in order to co-operate with God in this work of sanctification. In order to do this we will focus on Colossians 3:1-17, which tells us how we are to live as Christian people in the light of what Christ has done for us.

The theme of the first four verses is that we must be consistent. Paul has told the Colossians already (2:12ff.) that something radical has happened to them: they have been raised with Christ. He now goes on to say that their lives are 'hidden with Christ in God...' (verse 3) and they must seek the things that are above, not earthly things. In other words, the Christian is to have a completely new perspective on life.

Christ is 'seated at the right hand of God' (verse 1) and he will supply all spiritual blessings, hence we must look to him. He is the 'fountain of blessing'. It is because he is seated at the right hand of God that we know of his right and power to bestow

gifts of grace. But this attitude of having our eyes
fixed on Christ and setting our hearts and minds
on the things above does not mean that we forget
about the everyday things of life and become
dreamers. The American commentator, William
Hendriksen, put it like this:

'Those that seek to obtain these "things that are
above" are not chasing phantoms but are gathering priceless treasures. They are not the kind of
people who forget about their duty in the here and
now. On the contrary, they are very practical, for
the graces (given to them) enable them not only to
gain victory upon victory in their struggle against
fleshly indulgence but also to be truthfully "the
salt of the earth" and "the light of the world".' [21]

We must be consistent, then, and live in accord-
ance with what has been done on our behalf. In the
remainder of the passage, Paul shows the precise
way in which we are to live and makes it clear that
there is both a negative and a positive side.

The Negative Side (verses 5-11)
We are to 'put to death' the things of the earthly
nature (verse 5) and we are to rid ourselves of various wicked and evil habits (verse 8). We have, according to Paul, 'taken off' the old self and 'put

---

21.William Hendriksen, *Colossians and Philemon*, Banner of Truth, 1964, pp.140,141.

on' the new self. The words used here for taking
off and putting on suggest the discarding of an old
coat and the replacing of it with a new one. The
idea is that the old coat no longer fits and therefore
we need a new one. Similarly, the old sins and vices
no longer 'fit' with our new life in Christ and therefore they must be discarded.

It is interesting to notice that all this talk about
taking off and putting on, about putting sins to death
and ridding ourselves of various things, comes
immediately after verses 1-4 which tell us to fix
our hearts and minds on the things above. Do you
see the point? Paul is saying that the best way to
remove sin and all its habits from our lives is to set
our hearts and minds on things above. That is very
important. We are not to concentrate on the sins
themselves, because that could easily be counter-
productive. Rather, we are to set our hearts and
minds on the virtues which we see in Christ. It is a
paradox, but by concentrating on the good things
we are at the same time dealing with the bad things.

But is there a confusion in Paul's mind in these
verses? If the believer has already died to sin and
to self and to the law (verse 3) why is he now told
(verse 5) to put certain things to death? The answer
lies in the difference between the believer's state
and his condition. His state is perfect – complete
in Christ, justified (pardoned and accepted) and
adopted into the family of God. But his condition
is still sinful. We have not yet become in ourselves

what we already are in Christ. This is all the more important because of the wrath of God. The things of verse 5 lead naturally to the wrath of God in verse 6. It cannot be otherwise. God hates sin and cannot countenance its presence. Someone has said that sin attracts God's wrath like a magnet. That is so. Hence the believers are urged to rid themselves of all sin. Thus in verses 9-11 the believers are told to continue to do in practice what they have already done in principle.

The Positive Side (verses 12-17)
Paul begins here by addressing the Colossians as 'God's chosen people, holy and dearly loved...'. William Hendriksen comments on this description:

> 'They have been cleansed by the blood of Christ from the guilt of their sins, and are being delivered, more and more, from sin's pollution, and renewed according to the image of God'. [22]

Having been told to 'take off' the old sins and vices, the Colossians are now told what to 'put on' (verses 12-14). One commentator, Alexander MacLaren, has called these qualities, 'the garments of the renewed soul'. [23] If the believers put on these things then the peace of Christ will rule in their

---

22. William Hendriksen, *Colossians and Philemon*, p.156.
23. Alexnder MacLaren, *Colossians and Philemon*, Hodder & Stoughton, pp.305-319.

hearts (verse 15) and the word of Christ will dwell in them (verse 16). This will lead to God-centred worship (verse 16) and to an attitude which involves doing everything in Christ's name (verse17).

Let us fill out this teaching a little by concentrating on what it means to put sin to death. The verses of Scripture which are most important to help us understand this are Romans 6:11-14. Romans 6 begins with an objector who responds to Paul's teaching about justification by saying, 'If God's grace so abounds when we sin, then why not go on sinning and let it abound!?' Paul's answer is to demonstrate in verses 5-7 that the nature of the new-born Christian is such that this is impossible. In the first place, we cannot go on sinning because we have died to that way of life and, in the second place, we don't want to go on sinning because we have a new love, a new master, a new way of living. The unbeliever who poses the question is not taking account of the most important factor of all – the new birth.

If it were possible for God to forgive all our sins, past, present and future, while leaving us precisely in our present sinful condition then this objection might well be valid. But when God changes our status (justification) he immediately goes on to change our condition (sanctification). To emphasise this point Paul, in verses 1-10, teaches that just as Christ died and then rose again, so we must die to sin and rise again in newness of life. We must not let sin reign nor must we give our bodies to sin.

Then, in verses 12-13 he produces two impera-
tives concerning the Christian life, and in verse 14
he asks us to recognise the fact that we are not under law but under grace. This means that the grace
of God has set us free from 'sin' as well as 'law'. If
this were not so then nothing would really have
changed. It would be pointless redeeming us and
giving us new birth if we were not also set free
from the control of sin.

In verses 15-23 we have an analogy from the
slave market. A slave must obey his master but there
comes a point when that obligation to obey is ended,
namely, when the slave dies. From that time on the
master can give whatever orders he pleases to the
corpse but it will pay no attention. Such, says Paul,
is our relationship to our old master 'sin'. The
illustration ends by telling us that not only is there
a difference in the character of the service required
by our new master, but the wages are different. The
wages of the one is eternal death whereas the wages
of the other is eternal life.

This, then, is a summary of Romans 6. In verses
1-14 we are taught that the believer's union with
Christ is the ground for the life of holiness in which
he is set free from the life of sin. In verses 15-23
we find this truth illustrated and applied.

In 1 Peter 4, Peter says much the same kind of
thing as Paul. Having already developed in the earlier chapters of his letter the argument that we must

live for God and not for ourselves, he now tells us that since Christ has suffered we ought to 'arm ourselves with the same attitude'. The reason he gives for this is very important to our present study: 'because he who has suffered in his body is done with sin'. He then goes on to say, 'As a result, he does not live the rest of his earthly life for evil human desires, but rather for the will of God'. He is simply putting in a different way the teaching of Romans 6:11-14. Peter then spells out the implications of this (verses 4-6). Notice also the implication in verse 7 that such a way of life is essential if we are to be able to pray.

What 1 Peter 4 and Romans 6:11-14 are saying is this: just as Christ was put to death, so we must put sin to death. In effect, we are to refuse to allow sin to exercise its power over us. Having been united to Christ, we share in Christ's victory over sin and death. He is our new master, and we have died as far as our old master, 'sin', is concerned. Sin can give us all kinds of instructions but we have died to sin and therefore cannot and must not obey. Alan Stibbs put it like this:

> '...because of Christ's death for them, those who become Christians cannot live the rest of their earthly lives as they did before.' [24]

---

24. A. M. Stibbs, *I Peter*, Tyndale Nerw Testament Commentaries, IVP, 1977, pp. 145-146.

This is all very well, but how does it work out in practice? Do we find ourselves able to put sin to death? Or do we find that the very same sins continue to trouble us day after day, week after week, month after month, year after year? If this is the way things are in our lives it cannot be because God is not able to sanctify us, it must rather be because we have resisted his will and resisted his Spirit. In other words, disobedience is at the root of the lack of sanctification in our lives.

Now this raises something of a problem. We rightly say that salvation from beginning to end is the work of God and that we contribute nothing to our salvation. Our good works are the result of grace not the cause of it and even these works are the result of grace acting by faith. But having said that, we must not play down the very important place given in Scripture to obedience and sheer effort on the part of the believer. This work is called *mortification*, which may be understood from a study of Romans 8:13, 2 Corinthians 7:1 and Colossians 3:5.

The Scottish theologian John Murray describes mortification in this way:

'This mortifying and cleansing process is concerned with sin and defilement still adhering to the believer, and it contemplates as its aim the removal of all defilement of flesh and spirit. Nothing less than the complete eradication of this sinfulness is compatible with the destination of the believer, namely, conformity to the image of God's

Son. He was holy, harmless, undefiled, and separate from sinners, and they must be like him.' [25]

The believer, then, is called to 'throw off the sin
that so easily entangles' and to 'make every effort
to be holy'. In other words *we* have to do something, we have to 'work out our salvation with fear
and trembling' (Philippians 2:12). James Philip, a
Church of Scotland minister in Edinburgh, sums it
up well:'The focal point where the divine work and
the human meet is obedience.' He then goes on to
say this, 'Obedience is the touchstone of every advance in the Christian life, just as every hindrance
in it is ultimately traceable to our disobedience or
our tardiness in obeying.'

This is a subject which sadly does not receive
the attention it deserves. This despite the fact that
there are many biblical passages which speak of
our unconditional obligations to work towards holiness, to be obedient and to grow spiritually by
submitting ourselves to God: Romans 6:11ff.; 12:1,
2; 2 Corinthians 7:1; Ephesians 4:22ff.; Colossians
3:12ff.; 1 Peter 1:15,16 and 2 Peter 3:11 are clear
examples of this.

We can say, then, that obedience is necessary
for growth and progress in Christian living. This
means that we must ask ourselves some searching
and pertinent questions. Do we feel that we have
made little or no progress in our Christian lives?

---

25. John Murray, *Collected Writings*, Vol.2, p.296.

Perhaps there is some area which we have not given over to God. Is there some moral failure or disobedience in our lives? Is there some sin from which we have never turned or repented? There, perhaps, is the impediment to spiritual growth.

Too many people today are not prepared to go this way of holy obedience and slow, but steady, spiritual growth. They want short-cuts or dramatic experiences. They want to be sanctified in an instant. They are not prepared to be disciplined by God or to submit to his way of holiness.

How, then, are we to put sin to death? What does it involve? We might put it like this: to put sin to death means to recognise those areas of our lives which are sinful and displeasing to God and, by his promised Holy Spirit, to change them. But we must be committed to this work of mortification. We are all prepared to admit to certain sins, to ask God's forgiveness for them and to seek to repent of them and do them to death. But it is often the case that the very sins which are most needing to be done to death are the ones we harbour and excuse.

The great Irish writer and scholar C.S. Lewis said that he never used to tell his mother when he had toothache because he knew that she would take him to the dentist. And he also knew that the dentist, when he had dealt with the tooth which was giving the pain, would then look at all the other teeth to see what needed doing to them! He tells us that he was quite happy for the dentist to deal with the tooth which was giving him pain but didn't want him to go near the others.

That story illustrates the problem very well. Before we can really begin to put sin to death we have to be willing to do so. Many of us secretly have no intention of fighting against sin in our lives because we are happy with ourselves the way we are. To be perfectly honest, there are even certain sins which we like and which we are not prepared to give up. In some respects we are quite happy, when God is deeply unhappy. Are there sins in our lives which are unrepented of and which we have made no effort to put to death? Are there sins which we have no intention of giving up? Then beware, because one day we must each face God. Our reasons for not dealing with each and every sin will sound pretty flimsy when we are standing in the presence of a holy God. Sins must be rooted out and destroyed!

Unfortunately the word 'mortification' has fallen into disuse in the Christian church and that largely because of a misunderstanding of its meaning. In the minds of many people it had become associated with those who, in the past, have deliberately punished their bodies in order to please God. We can think of the hermits who lived in appallingly spartan conditions, refusing to eat properly or even to wear warm clothing because they wrongly believed that by punishing themselves in this way they would somehow get nearer to God.

But we must not be negative about the doctrine of mortification because of these errors. The early eighteenth century biblical commentator Matthew Henry said, 'The beginning of all true mortification lies in the mind, not in penances and hardships upon the body.' In other words, we don't become more holy simply by doing outward things. This does not, of course, mean that we should not put checks upon our bodily appetites and deal with outward sins, but it does mean that mortification is part of the inner struggle for control, the spiritual battle as described in Ephesians 6, which we are to consider in our next chapter.

Even in the new born believer, the remnants of the old self, or the old nature remain. This continues to struggle with us and in us. It was only because Christ died that he was able to conquer sin, and it is only in dying to self and to sin that we can live holy Christian lives. A candle is able to give light to the house only because it melts and becomes nothing. Similarly, if we are to be the light of the world, we must die to ourselves. In 1 Corinthians 15:31 Paul says, 'I die every day...' What he meant was that every day he consciously rejected the way of sin and death and instead chose the way of life. He did every day what God wanted and not what he wanted.

It is fairly easy to describe all this, but it is quite another thing to put it into practice, not least because it is so costly. Imagine that you are a slave and that for 24 hours each day, seven days a week, you are entirely at the disposal of your master, always having to do exactly what you are told. That gives a picture of true Christian discipleship but with one major difference. The slave would in most instances rather be free, but the Christian finds true fulfilment and freedom in obedience. As the hymn says:

> Make me a captive Lord,
> and then I shall be free;
> Force me to render up my sword,
> and I shall conqueror be.
> I sink in life's alarms
> when by myself I stand;
> Imprison me within thine arms,
> and strong shall be my hand.
>
> My will is not my own
> Till thou hast made it thine;
> If it would reach a monarch's throne
> It must its crown resign;
> It only stands unbent,
> Amid the clashing strife,
> When on thy bosom it has leant
> And found in thee its life.

Have you ever nursed an elderly relative through a long illness, or watched others do so? After a while you notice something. Those doing the nursing become so concerned with the patient and so caught

up in the well-being of the patient that they cease
to think about themselves. They don't take enough
sleep in case the patient needs them. They don't
worry about their own appearance but always make
sure the patient is comfortable and tidy. They lose
themselves as they care for someone else. That is
not a perfect illustration but it does draw attention
to the fact that the way of Christ is the way of self-
sacrifice, the way of surrender, the way of mortification.

Our prayer must be in the words of another
hymn:

> Is there a thing beneath the sun
> That strives with thee my heart to share?
> Ah! tear it thence, and reign alone,
> The Lord of every motion there;
> Then shall my heart from earth be free,
> When it has found repose in thee.

Chapter 10

SPIRITUAL WARFARE

Everything we have said about putting off the old life and putting on the new requires effort. Indeed, the Bible tells us that in a very real sense we are engaged in a battle. The most striking passage in the Bible on this subject is Ephesians 6:10-24, which speaks of the need for us to serve as soldiers of Christ.

Ephesians was a letter written by Paul from prison, probably in Rome and towards the end of his ministry. Paul went to Ephesus during his third missionary journey, the beginning of which is described in Acts 18:23. He stayed in Ephesus for almost three years (AD 52-55) and that stay is described in Acts 19:8-10. About five years after his stay in Ephesus, Paul writes to them about Christ. This letter is one of the finest expositions of the Christian gospel that we possess and, in Paul's own work, second only to Romans as a systematic statement of the Christian faith.

As is the case with most of Paul's writing, the first part of the letter is largely doctrinal and the second part is largely practical. That is to say, having spelled out the truth in the early part of the letter he then goes on to apply that truth in the later

part. In chapters 1-3 he describes the great transformation which had taken place in the lives of his
readers. Having been spiritually dead they were now
alive in Christ Jesus. He then goes on in chapters
4-6 to draw out the consequences of this. He deals
with such topics as patience, unity, telling the truth,
anger, stealing, unwholesome talk, brawling, slan-
der, sexual immorality and drunkenness. He then
speaks to different groups to explain the consequences of the gospel for their particular situation:
to wives and husbands, to children and parents, to
slaves and masters.

It is after he has done all of this that he writes
chapter 6:10-24, a fact that has two important lessons for us. Firstly, what Paul says about the devil
here is not meant to be theoretical and philosophi-
cal, but practical. Secondly, what he says about spiritual warfare and the enemy is to be read in the
context of all that he has already said about salvation.

Background (verses 10-13)
With that background and introduction let us consider Ephesians 6:10-13. There are a number of
points here to which we must give attention.

1. Strong in the Lord
In verse 10 Paul does not merely say 'be strong'
but 'be strong in the Lord and in his mighty power'.
There is a crucial difference. Our strength is not to

be found in ourselves, not even in our renewed and sanctified nature, but only in the Lord. We are constantly to be drawing strength from him. How often we fall down on this in practice! On a human level we try to be self-reliant and tend to draw on the resources and power of God only when we're in a situation we cannot handle with our natural human resources. This is a reflection of the basic sin of mankind which led to the Fall. If my youngest son, Christopher, were to get up tomorrow morning and say, 'Dad, I've decided that I don't need your help any more. I'm going to get by on my own. Please allow me complete independence and don't interfere unless I call on you', I would be surprised and saddened. Surprised because he's only nine (!), and saddened because I know that he couldn't cope on his own and really needs his parents' help. Imagine, then, how God feels when we try to manage in our own power instead of his.

2. The Full Armour of God

In verse 11 we are told to 'Put on the full armour of God so that you can take your stand against the devil's schemes'. This gives us the other side of the picture. Having drawn all our strength from God we then have to exercise that strength in the spiritual battle in which all Christians are, or ought to be, engaged. God, as it were, gives us all the armour and weaponry (both offensive and defensive) which is required for the battle but *we* have to do the fighting. In a very real sense the fight against the devil is our fight, but God arms us and we draw our strength from him.

Notice, however, that we are to put on '...the full armour of God...', not just part of it. We must not be undefended at a single point. We won't develop this thought here because shortly we shall be looking at the armour in more detail but do bear in mind this important truth: God has furnished us with all that we require in order to fight and to win this spiritual battle and if we go into battle unprepared or ill-equipped, it is not God's fault, but ours.

3. The Devil's Schemes
The reason for putting on the armour is to take a stand 'against the devil's schemes'. What does Paul mean by this? What are the 'devil's schemes'? The well-known biblical scholar F.F. Bruce gives a good answer:

> '...the stratagems by which the supreme enemy endeavours to gain an advantage over the people of God in their spiritual warfare'. [26]

We live in an age which would prefer to believe that there is no force of evil in the world, and in which even some who concede that there is such a force reject the view that we should conceive of it in personal terms. It has been said that the greatest

---

26. F. F. Bruce, *The Epistle to the Ephesians*, Pickering & Inglis, 1977, p.127.

victory the devil has won in modern times is to persuade people that he does not exist. But he does exist. We know that from the Bible and from experience. And the stratagems which the devil uses today are no different from the ones he has always used. Let us note just three of these.

First, he does everything he can to make us sin. He knows us well. He knows our weaknesses and he exploits them mercilessly. Do *we* know our weaknesses, those areas where we are most likely to succumb to temptation and sin? The devil does and attacks each of us accordingly.

Second, he tries to break down our belief in Christianity. Have you noticed how difficult it is to set aside a time each day for prayer and study of the Bible without it being constantly interrupted? Have you noticed how difficult it is to settle down to read a good solid Christian book? Have you noticed how the media insidiously presents an alternative worldview to that based on Christian truth?

Third, he tries to instill in us values, ambitions and a lifestyle which are not conducive to Christianity. There is great pressure on us to conform to the standards of the world but we must not allow this to happen. We must develop a Christian mind and a Christian lifestyle. Just because the consensus in our society says that something is right does not make it right. It is no fun swimming against the current of popular opinion and practice but that is what God calls us to do.

4. Our Struggle

In verse 12 Paul says that our struggle is not against flesh and blood but against the spiritual forces of evil. It is possible to give lip service to this yet show by our action that we do not believe it. This is most obvious in the matter of prayer. Church prayer meetings are often poorly attended, even in evangelical churches. If we really took seriously what we say we believe about the forces of evil then prayer would play a far greater part both in our lives and in the lives of our congregations.

This does not, of course, mean that we develop an unhealthy obsession with evil and the supernatural as some have done. There are Christians who see demons and devils on every corner and in some quarters exorcism has become more popular than Bible study. There must be balance in our thinking, but we ignore or play down the malevolence of the devil at our peril. Paul makes it clear in verse 13 that we must stand our ground. The reason for putting on the armour is that we might stand firm in the day of evil.

This does not mean, however, that we are in any danger of losing our salvation. Paul began in chapter 1 by telling us that God chose us before the creation of the world and that he works out everything in conformity with the purpose of his will. That being the case we can face the devil with confidence because he cannot ultimately destroy us. God has already determined the outcome of the battle, and, as Jesus assures us in John 10:29, none can pluck us from the Father's hand. This is the doctrine of *the perseverance of the saints*, which assures us that once you are a Christian you are a Christian for life and your salvation cannot be lost.

The Christian Armour (verses 14-24)
Paul now gives six aspects of the armour without which a Christian dare not go into battle:

1. The Belt of Truth (verse 14)
For the Roman soldier the belt was crucial. It was the piece of his equipment which held everything together. His garments were bound by the belt, and even his sword was hung from it. It is not insignificant, then, that Paul begins his analogy by speaking about 'truth'. Truth, he is saying, is the foundation and support for everything else. If we do not have the truth then none of the rest of the armour will do us any good because it will not fit properly together.

Here is the first point at which we must be well-protected against the enemy. We must know the truth and we must be able to defend the truth. This does not mean that we have to be acquainted with the intricacies of theology, but we do need to know our Bibles and to understand something of how all of what we read in the Bible fits together. We must also remember that the devil is a liar (see John 8:44). To know and believe the truth is an important protection against him.

Notice, however, that it is not sufficient to know the truth; we must also believe it. The devil himself knows the truth but that does not alter his condition. Do you believe the truth found in the Bible, or do you have major doubts and hesitations? It is precisely in these areas that the devil will attack you. All the more reason, then, why Christians must come to a clear and firm persuasion of the truth.

One important element in this is that the Christian faith does not claim to be one way to God among others, it claims to be the *only* way. By its very claims it passes judgement upon all other supposed ways to God. Some may regard this as arrogant but it is really a question of integrity. Those who say that there are many ways to God, Christianity included, are devaluing truth. If Christianity says one thing and another religion says the opposite then there is a contradiction involved in attempting to argue that really we are saying the same thing in different ways.

When Jesus says, 'No-one comes to the Father except through me' (John 14:6) and liberal theologians say that there are many ways to God, we have a conflict. When Luke, writing about the Lord Jesus Christ, tells us, 'There is no other name under heaven given to men by which we must be saved' (Acts 4:12) and others tell us that we can just as easily be saved through other religions or philosophies, there is a conflict. It simply will not do to pretend that there is no conflict and that we are all saying the same thing in different ways.

There can be no compromise on this fundamental issue – Christianity claims to be the truth about God. It can be accepted or it can be rejected, but it cannot be harmonised with other religions, or made into a contribution towards debate. It must stand as it is.

2. The Breastplate of Righteousness (verse 14)

Most of Paul's letter to the Romans, and a considerable part of the remainder of his writings, is given over to the question 'How can I be right with God?' Or, to put the question another way, 'How can I be justified in the sight of God?' (The Greek words for 'righteousness' and 'justification' are basically the same.) As we have seen in chapter 4, being righteous or justified in the sight of God is the fundamental distinguishing doctrine of the Christian faith.

It is important that each of us becomes familiar with what the Bible says about justification. Review chapter 4 of this book so that you will be able to give someone who is not a Christian a clear statement on the meaning and significance of justification as taught in the New Testament.

3. Feet Fitted With The Readiness That Comes From The Gospel of Peace (verse 15)

Paul may have two thoughts in mind here. Firstly, he wants us to be firm of foot and not easily slip. But secondly, and more importantly, he desires that

every Christian be the willing and enthusiastic
bearer of good news. Sadly that is not always the
case. There are many people who claim to be Christians but who refuse to go out and tell people about
Jesus. They make Christianity into a private matter
of communion between the individual and God.
That is all wrong. The Christian faith is good news.
It is a message, and by its very nature it must be
taken out and told to the world. It cannot be kept
under wraps. When God came to the first disciples
in the power of the Holy Spirit on the Day of Pen-
tecost they did not continue to hide in their upper
room. Instead, they spilled out on to the streets of
Jerusalem to tell everyone that Jesus Christ was
alive and that there was good news for all who
would come to him in faith and repentance. Like-
wise, we ought to be ready to share the good news.

4. The Shield of Faith (verse 16)

The word 'faith' can be used in at least two ways.
There is the faith that leads to justification which
we can call 'saving faith', and there is the faith by
which we live day by day, trusting God. Since the
faith spoken of in this verse has as its purpose the
extinguishing of the flaming arrows of the evil one,
I take it that Paul is speaking not of the initial step
of faith which leads to salvation, but of the day to
day exercise of faith in our battle against the devil.
This being the case, notice that the shield does not
only stop the darts, it extinguishes them!

If you have faith in God then you will be strong and the enemy will not gain a foothold. It is the easiest thing in the world to doubt, but it is the most comforting and joyful thing in the world to believe. Christians sometimes agonise over problems of minor significance and get quite overwrought about unimportant things. But if we believe that there is an all-powerful, personal God who created the whole world, who loves his children with a love which took him to the cross, and who is concerned with every single detail of our lives then there is no place for worry. Paul, in Philippians 4:6 said, 'Worry about nothing, instead pray about everything' (Living Bible translation). But we do worry, don't we? Perhaps the extent to which we worry is the extent to which our faith needs to be strengthened. We must take seriously God's promises to be with us, to guide us and to support us.

5. The Helmet of Salvation (verse 17)

In 1 Thessalonians 5:8 Paul writes about putting on the 'hope of salvation as a helmet'. What does he mean? I think he means that the hope of salvation and the hope of eternal life is our protection against the enemy. In other words, if we are sure that we cannot fall from salvation, that none can pluck us from the Father's hand and that our salvation is guaranteed and assured because it is by grace, then we are protected from the enemy.

The expression is also found in Isaiah 59:17

where it is God himself who wears the breastplate
of righteousness and the helmet of salvation.

6. The Sword of the Spirit (verse 17)

All the other parts of the armour are intended for
our protection, but Paul now turns to a weapon of
attack. There is no defence against this sword,
whether it is used against the enemy or even against
ourselves (look up Hebrews 4:12)! Like any other
weapon we need to become familiar with it before
we can use it. Like any other weapon we need to be
confident about what it can do before we use it. To
help gain this confidence, notice what Scripture
says about its own origin and purpose in 2 Timothy
3:16 and 2 Peter 1:21.

As we think about the fact that the Word of God
is our sword with which to do battle against Satan,
it is instructive to remember that this is precisely
what Jesus did when he was tempted, as described,
for example, in Matthew 4. Three times in that passage we find Jesus telling Satan, 'It is written'. This
was his sword against the enemy, and it won him
the victory. Incidentally, we find the devil in that
same story quoting Scripture back at Jesus in order to tempt him. It is very important for us to recognise this. The devil uses Scripture maliciously
for his own ends. Bear that in mind the next time
someone uses the Bible to prove something which
is manifestly absurd or heretical.

In verses 18-20 Paul makes a strong plea for

prayer. In one sense we might say that this is the other weapon which, along with Scripture, is to be used in the Christian's struggle against the world, the flesh and the devil. This helps to confirm Paul's conviction that Christians are soldiers engaged in warfare, and must be properly armed and trained in the things of God. And, amongst other things, they must 'be alert' (verse 18).[27]

---

27. For further discussion of Spiritual Warfare, see David Searle, *Be Strong in the Lord*, Christian Focus Publications, 1994; and James Philip, *Christian Warfare and Armour*, Christian Focus Publications, 1989.

Chapter 11

PERFECTIONISM

We must now consider a theological error which has sometimes led to a complete misunderstanding of how holiness is obtained, and then see how that same error is prevalent today in some theological circles.

As we saw when looking at Romans 6, Paul deals with the subject of freedom from sin. In chapter 7, he returns to a discussion of the place of the law which he had previously touched upon in 2:12-16 and in 3:19-22. There is a parallel between what he says about sin in chapter 6 and what he says about the law in chapter 7. In chapter 6 he has argued that we are set free from sin and therefore it has no power over us. He now produces the same argument with respect to the law.

In Romans 7, Paul addresses what he has to say to two people. Firstly, he addresses the man who is so concerned with the law that he has become a legalist, not understanding the proper relationship between the Christian and the law. The theologians call him a 'neonomian', one who erects a new law for Christians. Secondly, Paul speaks to the man who believes that the law has no significance for him whatsoever because he is a Christian, and who deliberately ignores or diminishes its teaching. He is what the theologians have called an 'antinomian'.

In verses 1-6 Paul speaks to the legalist or neonomian. He insists that the law no longer exercises lordship over the Christian because we have been delivered from it by the death of Christ. Our bondage is to Christ, not to the written code. We have been discharged from our obligation to the law, indeed we have died to it. We are now living the new life in the Spirit. This means that Christian obedience becomes, not an externally imposed obedience to some written law, but an inner obedience to God. There is all the difference in the world between those who obey God because of a sense of duty or obligation or fear of hell, and those who serve him willingly because the Spirit has made them willing.

In verses 7-13 Paul turns his attention to the other man, the one who would be rid of the law altogether, the antinomian. He tells this man that the law is good and that the problem lies in sinful actions. What Paul had just said to the legalist might have mistakenly led some to believe that the law is a bad thing, but Paul wants to make it clear that he is not saying this. The law is holy (verse 12) but sin uses the law for its own ends, and so produces sin.

In verses 14-25 we come to the main section for our present purposes. Having spoken to the neonomian and the antinomian, the legalist and the lawbreaker, Paul now turns to address the person who has struck the proper balance, the law-abiding believer. This is the one who trusts in Christ alone for salvation but who recognises the value of the law in demonstrating how he ought to live. In this passage Paul deals with the inner conflict of the believer. The autobiographical picture which Paul paints in these verses is one with which all Christians should identify. We try to live as Christians but so often we fail. Paul is very open and honest about this. The good things we want to do we fail to do, and the evil things we don't want to do are often the very things we find ourselves doing.

Perfectionism

Yet in spite of what Paul says here, there are some scholars who argue that in these verses he is describing his experience before he was converted. These scholars believe that a Christian can know sinless perfection while still in the body. They argue that a Christian can be so completely and entirely sanctified, so utterly holy, that he might never sin again. Most Christians do not believe this today but we must take the time to show that such teaching is utterly false because in certain Christian circles a theology which speaks of the need for believers to have a 'second blessing' experience is either directly or indirectly founded upon such a mistaken view.

It is important to notice that, from verse 14 on-wards, Paul uses the present tense. Therefore, those who interpret these words as being a description of Paul's pre-conversion experience do so simply in an effort to substantiate their argument. That argument would run as follows: Paul could not possibly have experienced this tension after he became a Christian because Christians are completely sanctified and therefore do not experience such tension. If that is true then I have never met a real Christian! Every believer I have ever met admits to this tension. Indeed, the whole tenor of Scripture supports the view that Christians *do* experience such tensions and battles. Our whole lives are portrayed in Scripture as a fight against the world, the flesh and the devil. Our lives are the territory upon which the great and ultimate battle between God and Satan is being fought. This is specifically stated, for example, in Ephesians 6:10-17.

In Romans 6:17 Paul says that it is not he who is sinning but 'sin' itself. He is making an important point here, not simply passing the blame for his sin to a third party. He is recognising the way things are in reality. Elsewhere in Scripture (for example, in Galatians 5:17) we find that we have a 'sinful nature' which continues to fight against the Holy Spirit who has taken up residence within us.

The fruit of the Holy Spirit will increasingly, we trust, be manifested in our lives, but sanctification goes on until the day we die. Indeed, Jesus tells us to die daily to our sins (Luke 9:23). If we could be completely holy and sanctified here and now, would such a command not be entirely meaningless? The writer to the Hebrews tells us that this struggle is not only a real part of the experience of every believer but that it is part of God's purpose for us as he seeks to discipline us and bring us to maturity in Christ (look at Hebrews 12:1-14).

James Philip sums up the whole thing very well:

'The Christian is called to live his new life in the old death-doomed environment. He is thus in a paradoxical situation, being both 'free from sin' and at the same time 'subject to the condition of sin'. Because he is both 'in Christ' and 'in the flesh' he is not able to be a sinner, and since this is so, there will always be tension and conflict in his experience.' [28]

As we saw in chapter 8, the Bible teaches that holiness is both an immediate act of God and a gradual process. There is an *initial* (or definitive) sanctification in which some of God's work of making us holy is accomplished the moment we are born again. There is also *progressive* sanctification by which God goes on making us holy until the day we die. But there are those who have taken a different view, one which has had such serious ef-

28. James Philip, *The Growing Christian*, Christian Focus Publications, 1992, p.47.

fects that we need to look at some examples of how it developed.

The Holiness Movement

In the first half of the 19th century, a movement began in the United States which was destined to become, in the words of American Presbyterian theologian Henry Van Dusen, 'the third force in Christendom'. One strand of this movement can be traced to C.G. Finney, a Presbyterian revival preacher who became a Congregational Professor of Theology at Oberlin College, Ohio. This college developed what has been called 'Oberlin theology', the main thrust of which was Christian perfectionism. Finney taught that baptism with the Holy Spirit was a second experience after conversion which brought power and holiness.

The other strand of this movement arose within the Methodist Church, due to a strong emphasis on John Wesley's teaching about 'entire sanctification'. This spread rapidly and Holiness Associations were formed to propagate the tenets of this theology. Holiness Associations in time became Holiness Churches and even Holiness denominations (such as the Church of the Nazarene).

At the beginning of the 20th century events occurred which meant that the holiness movement broke into two distinct and separate camps. On the one hand the Wesleyans continued the original teaching of the holiness movement, emphasising the need for a 'second blessing' which would bring entire sanctification. On the other hand the Pentecostal movement came into being. The beginnings of the Pentecostal movement can be traced to a Bible School, Bethel College, which began in Topeka, Kansas, in 1901. For most Pentecostals, however, the key event was a phenomenon called 'the Azusa Street experience' of 1906 when the Apostolic Faith Gospel Mission was born. From then until now Pentecostal churches have spread rapidly.

Like the Wesleyans, the Pentecostals affirmed that baptism with the Holy Spirit was a second experience, subsequent to conversion, but they added that the evidence of this baptism was the gift of speaking in tongues. Some Pentecostals continue to believe in entire sanctification, but most do not. The main theological view which unites Wesleyans and Pentecostals is that a second experience after regeneration is required. For the Holiness movement the second experience is said to bring complete sanctification, for the Pentecostal movement it is said to bring power and the supernatural gifts of the Holy Spirit.

The modern Charismatic movement consists of those who have accepted the main principles of this 'second-blessing theology' but who have either chosen to remain within the established denominations, or who have formed house-churches and independent fellowships. The important point for our study is to understand that the very existence of Holiness, Pentecostal and Charismatic movements has come about because of a faulty view of holiness and sanctification. This is why it is so important to understand what the Bible teaches about holiness and sanctification.

Mainstream Christianity in this country has been affected by second-blessing theologies through the influence of the well-known Keswick Convention, held every summer in the Lake District, and organisations such as the Faith Mission. Most Keswick speakers today do not believe in a second blessing for sanctification, nor do all Faith Mission personnel, but we must be aware of the dangers inherent in this position. Holiness is only to be obtained in the face of difficulty, struggle, opposition and discipline.

Yet do the scriptures not tell us to be perfect? What are we to make of Matthew 5:48, 2 Corinthians 7:1, 13:2 and Hebrews 6:1? The answer lies in the fact that, although we are urged to aim for perfection, there is not the slightest suggestion in these verses or elsewhere in Scripture that any believer will attain to that while in the body. Indeed, all the evidence seems to be against this. Consider, for example, 1 John 1:8,10 and the testimonies of others: Isaiah 6:5ff.; Daniel 9:4-9; Ephesians 3:8 and 1 Timothy 1:15.

The nineteenth century evangelical Anglican bishop, J.C. Ryle, put it like this:

'In face of such facts as these I must protest against the language used in many quarters, in these last days, about *perfection*. I must think that those who use it either know very little of the nature of sin, or of the attributes of God, or of their own hearts, or of the Bible, or of the meaning of words.' [29]

Are you struggling in your Christian life? Are you fighting and battling against sin and do you sometimes feel that you are making no progress? Do you have good intentions and then see yourself doing precisely the opposite of what you intended to do? And does that sometimes make you feel as if you can hardly be a Christian at all? Then take heart from the story of Paul's own struggles and remember that even the very act of fighting against the world, the flesh and the devil constitutes strong evidence that you are on God's side.

As Christians, we can never forget that we have an enemy, one so powerful that he is called in Scripture 'the god of this age' (2 Corinthians 4:4). This enemy hates God and detests all talk of Christ. His great objective is to destroy the church of God. In this work he cannot be ultimately successful because the victory belongs to Christ. Our great enemy will one day be thrown into the lake of fire prepared for himself and his angels. We must never forget that we are more than conquerors through Christ.

---

29. J.C. Ryle, *Holiness*, James Clarke and Co. p.xi.

This in no way minimises the fierceness of the struggle and the heat of the battle. But it is a battle already won, and we must therefore persevere to the end. There is no perfection in holiness in this world, only a target at which to aim. The enemy is determined to keep us as far from that target as he is able. Are we equally determined to resist him in every way we can? We have the assurance in Scripture that if we do so he will flee from us (look up James 4:7).

Chapter 12

WITHOUT HOLINESS NO-ONE
WILL SEE THE LORD

We have said a good deal about the holiness which results from the new birth, but we cannot leave the subject without saying perhaps the most important thing of all, namely, that without holiness no-one will see the Lord. We can put this another way: the Bible tells us that there is a pre-requisite for entrance to heaven and that pre-requisite is holiness.

Hebrews 12

Our chapter title is taken from Hebrews 12:14: 'without holiness no-one will see the Lord' and it is important to put that statement in its context. Hebrews 12 begins with the word 'therefore', demonstrating that there is a connection with what has gone before. The connection can be stated in this way. In chapter 11 the writer has described the great heroes of faith. Here in chapter 12 he is telling us that we must not give up when things are hard in the Christian life but take encouragement from the example of these great men and women of God and persevere to the end.

The imagery used in 12:1-2 is that of the Olympic Games. The Old Testament saints are pictured as spectators who have already completed the race, while we are still running. They are cheering us on, as it were. Not only are these godly spectators cheering us on, however, but Christ himself is ahead of us. We are to fix our eyes on him, be encouraged by those who have triumphed, and press on to win the race. But what does the writer mean by this imagery? What is this race in which we are running? The answer is to be found in verse 1: 'Let us throw off everything that hinders and the sin that so easily entangles...'. What the writer is referring to is life itself and the battle against all that is sinful and wicked. This is supported by verse 4 which speaks of '...your struggle against sin...'. He is dealing with the importance of putting to death all that is sinful so as to win the race of life.

In verses 4-11 the writer speaks of God's discipline. It is clear from these verses (especially verse 7) that the Hebrews were suffering hardship for the sake of the gospel, and the writer is concerned to teach them that this is all to the good. Just as a human father disciplines his children, so God disciplines us. Discipline is never a pleasant thing when administered but afterwards we shall be able to look back on it with gratitude for it will have made of us better people.

Hebrews 12, then, is concerned with holiness. In verse 10 we read, 'God disciplines us for our good, that we may share in his holiness'. The end product of hard times and hard suffering for the sake of Christ and his gospel is holiness. In our own day it is not insignificant that believers who lived and suffered behind the former Iron Curtain are in the main more Christ-like, more holy, and more godly than believers in our land. Why? Because they have been refined by the fires of persecution and hardship. This is precisely what Hebrews 12 would lead us to expect. In verse 11 we are told that God's discipline '...produces a harvest of righteousness and peace for those who have been trained by it'.

In verses 14-29 the writer exhorts his readers to holy living, reminding them that they are the people of the New Covenant. In verse 25 he concludes that if the people of the Old Covenant suffered when they refused to listen to God's Word, then our punishment for a similar failure will be that much greater because more has been revealed to us. This principle that the more we have received the more that will be expected of us is taught also in the parable of the talents which Jesus told at Matthew 25:14-30.

The key verse in this chapter is verse 14: 'Make every effort to live in peace with all men and to be holy; without holiness no-one will see the Lord'. Notice carefully the two points the writer is making here. The first is that we are to 'make every effort to be holy'. As we have already seen, obedience and mortification are very important aspects of any biblical presentation of Christian holiness. They constitute the other side of the picture from the divine work in sanctification. The second part of the statement, and our main concern in this present chapter, is that 'without holiness no-one will see the Lord'. This is perhaps the most important thing to be said in the whole study of Christian holiness. Here is the ultimate dividing line between those who are Christians and those who are not. Yet even this fundamental truth has been challenged.

In 1720, Principal James Hadow of St. Andrews accused Thomas Boston and his associates of teaching that holiness was not necessary for salvation. This arose in the context of what has become known as the 'Marrow' controversy. In fact the 'Marrowmen' (as they were called) did not play down the significance of holiness. They were simply protesting against a legalism which suggested that by obedience and works one could earn salvation. It is nonetheless interesting that such an accusation was made, because there is one sense in which it should always be made when the gospel is faithfully preached. That is to say, we should always emphasise the free offer of the gospel and insist that we contribute nothing to our salvation.

When we teach that holiness is essential for salvation, then, we must choose our words carefully. In affirming that holiness is essential for salvation we are not suggesting that anyone who tries to live a holy life will be saved. As we have already seen, to teach that righteousness can be obtained by works is legalistic and heretical.

When we say that holiness is essential for salvation we are saying that a true believer will be a holy person because that is what the Holy Spirit will make him. If holiness does not increasingly mark the life of the believer then we have every right to question whether the person concerned is a Christian in the first place. As you can see, we have to tread a very careful line here between suggesting salvation by works on the one hand, and playing down the importance of holiness on the other.

All the various doctrines of grace sit together in a balanced and ordered way and hence we must beware lest we upset the balance by stressing a doctrine more than it is stressed in Scripture, particularly if we do so at the expense of some other vital truth.

Fitted for Heaven
Holiness, then, is necessary for entrance to heaven. We can also say that someone who is not holy would not enjoy heaven! J.C. Ryle put it like this:

'Suppose for a moment that you were allowed to enter heaven without holiness. What would you do? What possible enjoyment could you feel there? To which of all the saints would you join yourself, and by whose side would you sit down? Their pleasures are not your pleasures, their tastes not your tastes, their character not your character. How could you possibly be happy, if you had not been holy on earth? ... I know not what others may think, but to me it does seem clear that heaven would be a miserable place to an unholy man. It cannot be otherwise. People may say, in a vague way, 'they hope to go to heaven;' but they do not consider what they say. There must be a certain 'meetness for the inheritance of the saints in light.' Our hearts must be somewhat in tune. To reach the holiday of glory, we must pass through the training school of grace. We must be heavenly-minded, and have heavenly tastes, in the life that now is, or else we shall never find ourselves in heaven, in the life to come.' [30]

Thomas Boston says much the same kind of thing and gives one devastating example:

'How would such as now account the Sabbath day a burden, brook the celebration of an everlasting Sabbath in the heavens!' [31]

When the Bible says, then, that without holiness no-one will see the Lord, it is underlining the fact that holiness is not only a qualification for entrance to heaven, but is also essential if we are to enjoy heaven.

---

30. J. C. Ryle, *Holiness*, James Clarke and Co., pp. 43-45.
31. Thomas Boston, *Works*, Vol.8, p.174.

The Work of the Spirit
So far in these studies we have stressed the neces-
sity of holiness, and we have seen both God's work
of sanctification, and our response in mortification and obedience. But there is one other area
which we must look at as we begin to draw these
studies to a close, namely, the importance of not
resisting the Holy Spirit. Scripture tells us that the
production of holiness in the life of the believer is
the main work of the Spirit. Look up what is said
in Acts 9:31; Romans 8:5; 14:17; 15:16; Galatians
5:16 and 5:22ff.. In this connection, Scripture also
gives us three specific directions. We are not to
quench the Spirit (1 Thessalonians 5:19), we are
not to grieve the Spirit (Ephesians 4:30) and we
are not to resist the Spirit (Acts 7:51). In pursuing
personal holiness, nothing is more important than
obeying these instructions.

Application
Much of what we have seen in our discussion of
holiness has been theological, that is to say, it has
involved the gathering together of various strands
of biblical teaching in order to point up some of
the doctrines of grace. But the material which we
have considered is also intensely practical, and I
want us now to examine ourselves and see in what
way God might be speaking to us through it.

We must ask ourselves the question: Am I holy?
Remember, without holiness no-one will see the

Lord. It is very important that we answer this question honestly and thoroughly. It will not do to say 'No, I am not holy. I am a sinner, but my sins have been forgiven'. That may well be true, but it is to avoid the question. Some Christians make no effort to be holy, believing it is impossible for them to be so. Such people must realise that God requires us to aim for holiness with effort and dedication, even though we never achieve that perfection.

We must not be casual about this matter. It is possible for us so to emphasise salvation by free grace, and the work of sanctification as a continuing process of God the Holy Spirit, that we do not sufficiently mourn and grieve over our sins. We must seek holiness with every atom of our being. We must be aware of how hateful and hurtful sin is to our holy God. We must also be conscious of how far we have to go in the way of grace. Remember, too, holiness is a practical thing, not a subject for mystics and monks. It is for all Christians without exception. It is just as necessary for a housewife, a factory worker, a student or a bank clerk to be holy as it is for a minister of the gospel. Holiness is concerned with very practical matters.

Assurance

Holiness is also a means towards assurance. There is a certain element of assurance in saving faith itself: if we did not believe that God was willing to save us we would not come to him. But there is

also assurance by what the theologians call the 're-
flex act', namely, that assurance which is to be had
by observing the work of the Holy Spirit in our
lives and witnessing the changes which he makes.

As we grow in grace and holiness and as God
changes us more and more into the image of Christ,
so our assurance deepens. We know what we were
when God found us and lifted us up and put our
feet on a rock, and we can see what we have become in Christ Jesus. We are still well aware of
how far we have yet to go, but our assurance deepens as we see God at work in our lives.

What is more, others can see God at work in
our lives. Did not Jesus say, 'By this all men will
know that you are my disciples, if you love one
another' (John 13:35)? Holiness is evidence of the
work of the Spirit of God, and that evidence helps
to bring assurance.

Holiness, then, is essential. If we are not Christians then there is a breach still existing between
ourselves and God. That breach is caused by our
sin. We are cut off from God because sinners cannot come into the presence of a holy God. If we
want to be right with God we must be holy. If we
are Christians and if we want to go to be with God
when we die, then holiness is essential. We must
be open to the Holy Spirit, allowing him free reign
to deal with our sinful lives and to bring them into
line with the life of Christ. We must also pray and
ask God to make us more holy and more Christlike

every day. In addition, we must be obedient to the Word of God and to the will of God.

Thomas Boston concluded a powerful sermon on sanctification with five inferences:

'1. Those who are unrenewed are unsanctified. Where there is no change of heart and life, there is no grace, 2 Cor.v.17. Ah! how many live as they were born, and are like to die as they live? They have no changes, but from evil to evil: no change from sin to holiness, and yet are unconcerned with their unrenewed state, sleeping until they sleep the sleep of death.

2. A partial change is not sanctification. Those who are changed, but not in the whole man, are not truly sanctified, but are yet in their natural pollution. Sanctification is not a new head full of knowledge, with the old heart and life; nor is it a new life, with the old heart and nature. But it is a change that goes through the whole soul and body, which must needs be followed with a new life, 2 Cor. v.17.

3. True sanctification puts work into the hands of the sanctified, that will occupy them while they live. Dying to sin, and living to righteousness, are works that will fill up every minute we have in the world.

4. Let none be so foolish as to sit down contented without sanctification, but study holiness as ever ye would see heaven. We want a title to heaven, we must get that in justification and adop-

tion: we want a meetness for heaven, and we must get that in sanctification. The sanctified are elected, and shall be glorified, 1 Pet.i.1,2,4 And they that live and die unsanctified, shall never see heaven, Heb.xii.14 'For without holiness no man shall see the Lord.'

5. Lastly, as ever ye would be holy, attend and improve the means of grace. Let not your afflictions drive you from God, neither be stupid under them, but fall in with the design of providence in them, for your sanctification.' [32]

As we come to the end of this chapter, I am conscious of how much we have not touched upon in this matter of Christian holiness. There is so much in Scripture which could have been brought to bear upon the subject and so many more areas which could have been touched upon. It is, however, my hope and prayer that the subject has been sufficiently opened out so as to cause each of us to earnestly examine our hearts and actively to seek holiness by the work of God the Holy Spirit in our lives.

---

32. Thomas Boston, *Works*, Vol.1, p.661.

Chapter 13

REGENERATION: WHERE DOES IT FIT IN?

We are now to consider where the doctrine of regeneration fits into the overall plan and purpose of God in the salvation of sinners. In chapters 1-12 we have examined individually some of the doctrines of the Christian faith. We must now try to explain how they fit together. It is rather like putting together a jigsaw, except that we human beings can never completely understand God's revelation and so any attempt at a systematic theology must always be tentative.

Of all the chapters, this will be the most complex and theological. It is also inevitable that there will be a certain amount of overlap with what has gone before. Nevertheless, it is probably the most important chapter for getting as complete a picture as possible of what God is doing when someone becomes a Christian. There has often been much confusion over the various terms which are used to describe the work of God in a person's life. Some people use words such as 'regeneration', 'conversion', 'justification' and 'effectual calling' without distinguishing properly between them and without being clear in their minds as to their relation with one another. Our purpose here is to try and clarify that situation. The following is an outline of the various themes we shall be dealing with in this chapter.

A. Romans 8:28-30
    1. Foreknew
    2. Predestined
    3. Called
    4. Justified
    5. Glorified

B. State and Condition

C. Regeneration
    1. Regeneration and Effectual Calling
    2. Regeneration and Conversion
    3. The Parts of Conversion
        (a) Repentance
        (b) Faith
    4. Regeneration and Justification
    5. Union with Christ
    6. Adoption
    7. Regeneration and Sanctification

A. Romans 8:28-30

I want us to begin by considering Romans 8:28-30. In these verses Paul takes several of the doctrines we have just mentioned and puts them in order. This is a good basis from which we can work to fit in the others which he does not mention here.

Paul begins this great passage with the rightly famous words of verse 28. This verse makes it clear that God acts in a special way ('works for the good') with respect to a particular group of people ('those who love him'). This does not in any sense take away from what the Bible says about the common grace of God, but it does say something special about this group of people who are described in two ways. They are the people who have been 'called by God', and they are those who 'love God'. From what we have seen so far it is clear that love for God can only exist where a sinner has been born again of the Spirit of God. This verse, therefore, is speaking about the regenerate and their place in God's plan.

The three verses which follow have been called the 'golden chain'. Indeed, the Puritan writer William Perkins called his volume of theology *A Golden Chaine* with specific reference to these verses. In other words, the doctrines mentioned here are all linked together and cannot be separated. Foreknowledge leads to glorification in an inexorable and infallible manner. One of the important implications of this is that we cannot lose our sal-

vation. Paul does not say that *some* of those God
foreknew will be called and *some* of them will be
glorified. The whole tenor of these verses is that
salvation is something God does by his grace and
that it is never in any doubt for those to whom it
refers.

Let us consider the five verbs Paul uses here.

1. 'Foreknew' - There has always been much discussion about the meaning of this word. There are
some who believe it means that God looked into
the future, saw those who would of their own free
will believe in Jesus Christ, and then decided that
all of those would be saved. But this destroys the
whole meaning and concept of foreknowledge and
makes a man's salvation dependent ultimately upon
his own decision. It also makes a mockery of any
proper understanding of the sovereignty of God
who, in this view, is only able to save those who
decide to believe in Jesus.

A proper understanding of this verse can be
obtained by reading John Murray's analysis of these
verses in his commentary on Romans.[33] Murray
explains that in the Bible the verb 'to know' can
have a variety of meanings. In particular, when it
says that God 'knows' someone, it implies that God
has a relationship with that person. Indeed, it often
seems to imply that God has 'set his love upon'
that person. For example, consider Matthew 7:23;

---

33. John Murray, *The Epistle to the Romans*, Eerdmans, 1965.

1 Corinthians 8:3; Galatians 4:9; 2 Timothy 2:19 and 1 John 3:1. If God's knowing someone means that he has set his love upon him, we can then say that 'those God foreknew' means 'those whom God set his love upon in advance'. This makes good sense in the context of the passage and, more importantly, it leaves God as the subject of the sentence, thus ensuring that salvation is by grace alone.

2. 'Predestined' - This biblical word means that those upon whom God set his love in advance he freely chose to save through Jesus Christ. All such will undoubtedly be saved, and no others. God is sovereign in salvation just as he was in creation. But as the verse makes clear, the ultimate object of predestination is not simply to determine where a person spends eternity but to bring that person into conformity to Christ. In one sense we might say that God's objective, from the time of the Fall in Genesis 3 until now, has been to take sinful men and women and remake them in the image of Christ. Predestination is God's means of achieving that objective.

3. 'Called' - This word is not referring to the 'external' call of the gospel which is issued every time the gospel is preached. We know this because the verse goes on to say that those God called he also justified, something which is not true of everyone who hears the gospel. Many people come under the sound of the gospel and are 'called' to believe in the Lord Jesus Christ, but most of them never respond to the offer of Christ and remain unregenerate.

If, as this passage says, every one who is called goes on to be justified, then this word 'called' must refer to what is known as the 'effectual call' of the Holy Spirit, the subject of our next chapter.

4. 'Justified' - This word dominates the thought of the early chapters of the epistle to the Romans, as we have already seen. Justification is a once-for-all irreversible decision by God to pardon and accept an individual sinner. It is an instantaneous act and not a process.

5. 'Glorified' - Finally, those God justifies he also glorifies. If we are Christians, we are to be glorified! Do we have any real conception as to what that means? Think of Moses coming down from the mountain with his face shining having been in the presence of God. Think of Jesus on the Mount of Transfiguration as he shone in glory. Think of the risen Christ in his new, glorified body. Scripture assures us that when he appears 'we shall be like him' (1 John 3:2). Words cannot express adequately what this means.

B. State and Condition

Before examining the various doctrines of grace and seeking to show their relation to regeneration it is important to pause and make one general observation to set the context. When a person is saved by grace there are two parallel operations taking place. The one concerns *his relationship to God*, and the other concerns *his nature and character*. The first of these is objective and concerns the sinner's 'state'; the second is subjective and concerns the sinner's 'condition'. In other words, salvation accomplishes two things: it changes a condemned man into one who is pardoned and justified, and it changes an unrighteous sinner into a holy child of God.

These two elements of salvation correspond to the two problems which man faces: guilt and pollution. It is not enough for a man to be pardoned, his nature requires to be changed. Man is a sinner, utterly cut off from God. Simply to pardon him without changing his nature would do no good. These two elements of salvation are usually dealt with under the broad headings of Justification and Sanctification.

God engages in a process to accomplish both elements of this required salvation. We describe this process in terms of various doctrines. There are doctrines which describe the change in the sinner's state: justification and adoption; there are doctrines which describe the change in the sinner's condi-

tion: regeneration, conversion, repentance and sanctification. And there are several doctrines which
overlap, including effectual calling, and union with
Christ. Our task is to see if we can unravel something of the meaning of each of these and see where
each fits into what is called the *ordo salutis*, the
order of salvation. To put it simply, what happens
first when I become a Christian, what happens last,
and what happens in between?

C. Regeneration

The first and most important thing to say is that
regeneration is the beginning of the process. It is
an act of God in which we do not co-operate or
have any active part. Just as I do not have any conscious part in my natural birth, so I do not have any
part in my second birth. It is from beginning to end
a work of God. He comes to a dead sinner and gives
new life. Both justification and sanctification begin here. Without this initial act of God in regenerating a dead sinner nothing else would happen. One
writer on this subject, Burkhardt, said:

> '...regeneration is the unrepeatable, once and for
> all, historical beginning of the new life. That is, it
> is the beginning of both justification and sanctifi-
> cation.' [34]

---

34. *The Biblical Doctrine of Regeneration*, Evangelical
Theological Monographs No.2, World Evangelical Fellowship Theological Commission, p.29.

Regeneration and Effectual Calling

The Westminster Confession of Faith, in keeping with much Reformed theology in the 17th Century, treats effectual calling and regeneration as being the same thing. It is, however, important that we distinguish between them. In the providence of God, his effectual call is always just that – effectual. The external call of the gospel is universal and says to every creature without exception, 'If you come to Christ in faith you will be saved'. In the mystery of God's sovereign election, however, not everyone is enabled to respond to that call, but only such as are effectually called. This is where regeneration comes in. What happens is that God regenerates the individual and enables him to understand the gospel, believe it and respond to the offer of Christ. But clearly, the effectual call is only effectual because of the regeneration which takes place. Without it the call would go unheeded.

Both Isaiah and Jeremiah were told that their words would go unheeded (look, for example, at Jeremiah 1:19). Why? Because God had determined to turn his face away from the people because of their sin. The preaching of the Word was not accompanied by regeneration and therefore it was not effectual for their salvation. Jonah did not want to go to Nineveh and took a fairly varied and interesting route before he preached to them. But when he did the result was overwhelming. Why? Because God gave the grace of regeneration as an accom-

paniment to the preaching of the Word, so making
it effectual. Paul was told to stay in Corinth longer
than he intended (Acts 18:9-11). Why? Because
God had some people in that city whom he had
determined would yet be born again. Paul was to
stay and preach the Word. In the cases of the individuals concerned that Word would be accompanied by regeneration and would, therefore, be effectual. In Acts 13:48 we are told that '...all who
were appointed for eternal life believed'. This
means that, in the cases of those so ordained by the
predestinating grace of God, the call of the gospel
was accompanied by regeneration, thus making it
effectual, with the result that they believed.

Regeneration and Conversion

We turn now to the most important distinction to
be made in this whole area, the distinction between
regeneration and conversion. These two are not the
same although they have often been used as inter-
changeable terms. Regeneration is an act of God
by which he brings new life to the soul. Conversion is our response to this, and has to do with the
exercise of repentance and faith. We might say, then,
that regeneration is God's work, and conversion is
our work. The former is what God does, and the
latter is what we are savingly enabled to do. Regeneration is not consciously known, but conversion is. Conversion is the proof that regeneration
has taken place.

Think for a moment about a man called Zacchaeus, whose story you can read in Luke 19:1-10. When he met with Christ he was born again of the Spirit of God. How do we know this? Because he 'converted', his life changed. The outward is the sign of the inward. Conversion is the evidence for the great work of regeneration which is invisible.

The Parts of Conversion

Let us now turn to a consideration of the two main parts of conversion. As Charnock rightly said, 'The first graces which appear in a renewed soul are repentance and faith',[35] and we need to be sure that we know what these graces are.

(a) Repentance

There is a common mistake which suggests that repentance is a condition of salvation. This error reveals itself in the kind of preaching which says that if you repent then you will be forgiven. This is not what the Bible says. The whole tenor of Scripture is that repentance is only possible after regeneration has taken place. How can a man repent if he is dead? And if repentance were to be a condition of salvation would that not take away from grace and therefore limit God? This is not to take away from those Scriptures which assert that repentance is necessary for salvation. What I am saying is that repentance flows from regeneration as a

---

35. Stephen Charnock, *Works*, Vol. 3, p.109.

result, rather than going before it as a cause.

It is the universal testimony of Reformed theology that repentance is a fruit of grace, something which is only possible precisely because God has made us alive in Christ. We could easily spend time proving this by looking at *The Westminster Confession of Faith* and the writings of great theologians like the Reformer John Calvin, and the Puritans John Owen and William Perkins.

(b) Faith

The other fruit of regeneration, which may properly be described as an aspect of conversion, is faith. When a person is brought to life by the regenerating grace of God he is given the gift of faith (Ephesians 2:8). Faith, in turn, is the instrument by which we lay hold on Christ for our justification. Faith is acceptance of the truth revealed to us by God and trust in Jesus Christ. It is important to notice that faith is the *result* of regeneration, but is the instrumental *cause* of justification. It is, therefore, the link which holds these doctrines together.

Regeneration and Justification

If regeneration is the first act of God in the transformation of a sinner's nature, justification is the first act of God in changing the sinner's state. The moment a man exercises the gift of faith to lay hold of Christ he is justified. This means that God passes a judgement to the effect that the individual is pardoned and forgiven. This involves all sins, past, present and future. It is as if God strikes out the sinner's name from the book listing all those who are sinners, heading for an eternity in hell, and writes the name instead in the Book of Life to be counted among the elect of God who will be with him in heaven one day. Regeneration, on the other hand, is not a judicial act of that sort, rather it is an act by which a man's life is changed. As a result, he thinks differently, he believes differently, he acts differently, he feels differently.

It is important to notice, however, that regeneration and justification are both vitally necessary and are connected in an unbreakable way, such that you cannot have one without the other. This does not mean, of course, that we are to risk confusing the two doctrines, or imagine that they are two ways of saying the same thing. They are separate and distinct aspects of the work of grace in the life of the individual.

Union with Christ

The first fruit of justification is union with Christ, but this union is only possible because regeneration has taken place. God could not join to Christ one who was still dead in the sinful pollution of an ungodly and unrighteous heart. God could not unite to Christ one whose nature had not been changed. Thus regeneration is a necessary prerequisite for union with Christ.

Adoption

If justification is the act of God by which he begins to change the sinner's state, adoption is the completion of that act. In adoption the sinner becomes a child of God through God's own saving grace, as we saw in chapter five.

Regeneration and Sanctification

Sanctification is the continuance of the work of regeneration in the soul. Although regeneration is a once for all act, sanctification is a process. Thomas Boston put it most helpfully when he explained that regeneration was the first act of sanctification. His description parallels what John Murray was later to say about definitive sanctification.

Calvin treated most of salvation under the broad general heading of sanctification in order to make the point that the entire purpose of God in salvation is to make man holy. This may sound simplistic, but if we think about it we can see what he means. When God created mankind it was for fellowship with himself. The Fall ruined that glorious purpose and so God had to start again, as it were. The purpose of salvation is to accomplish that same end, namely, to have a people who will freely worship and serve him. But there is a problem. Sinners cannot come in to the presence of a holy God. It is horrific even to contemplate such a thing. The problem, therefore, is how to make people holy and righteous enough to accomplish this purpose. Thus, in a sense, we can say that the whole purpose of God since the Fall has been the preparation of a sanctified people. Although sanctification has come at the end of this trip through the doctrines of grace it is the most important because it is the end for which God has been aiming since the events of Genesis 3.

All of this can be summed up in one sentence (and no doubt you wish I had told you that at the beginning!): Experience regeneration and everything else will follow. When we are born again of the Holy Spirit of God our conversion begins. On the one side this involves faith which leads to justification, union with Christ and adoption. On the other hand it involves repentance which leads to sanctification.

Chapter 14

HOW DOES IT HAPPEN?

Despite everything that we have considered so far, one fundamental question remains: How does this salvation, which God has provided for his people through the death of Christ, become a personal reality in the lives of individual men and women? It is clearly one thing to say that God has set his love upon us and chosen us, and Christ has died for us, but quite another thing to understand how that salvation experimentally becomes yours and mine.

We are now going to explore this question by taking a much closer look at the subject of 'effectual calling' which we introduced briefly in the last chapter.

When looking at Romans 8:29-30, we recognised that the crucial question is what the word 'called' means in these verses. We also noted that the clear teaching of these verses is that *all* those who are included at the beginning of verse 29 reach the end of verse 30! In terms of our subject, this means that all those who are called will be glorified. The implication of this, as we saw, is that when Paul speaks of those who are 'called', he cannot simply be referring to those who have heard the outward call of the gospel, because many of those who hear the external call of the gospel do not respond to it, and will ultimately be lost. It must instead refer to a 'calling' which is guaranteed to achieve its objective, namely, the glorification of those whom God has chosen. The 'call' in Romans 8:30, then, is an effectual call, a call which always and inevitably achieves its purpose.

The 19th century Princeton theologian Charles Hodge, in his commentary on these verses, says that the word 'called' refers to those whom God 'leads by the external invitation of the gospel, and by the efficacious operation of his grace, to the end to which they are destined.'[36] Plumer, in his commentary, spells it out even more clearly, 'That the calling here spoken of is not a mere invitation to the gospel feast, but an effectual persuasion and enabling of the soul to embrace Christ is clear from the connection and from the ordinary use of the word.' [37]

Effectual calling, then, is the act of God by which he combines the outward call of the gospel with an inner persuasion, such that men and women are enabled savingly to believe in the Lord Jesus Christ. It is no coincidence that the Greek word for 'church' used in the New Testament means those who are 'called out'. Effectual calling is the means by which God brings men and women into his kingdom and into a saving experience of Christ.

36. Charles Hodge, *Romans*, Banner of Truth, 1975, p.286.
37. William S. Plumer, *Romans*, Kregel, 1971, p. 426.

In order to consider this doctrine in more detail I have divided the material up into five sections.

1. The Fact of Effectual Calling

It is clear from Scripture that salvation is *by* grace *through* faith. This in itself helps to underline the fact that salvation is not achieved by a human decision but by an act of God. There are a number of passages of Scripture which support this view. Ephesians 2:1-5 describes the great transformation which has taken place in the life of every believer and attributes this change to the gracious activity of God. 2 Timothy 1:8,9 says much the same kind of thing. In both passages it is clear that God takes the initiative and accomplishes the salvation. Titus 3:3-7 emphasises the work of the Holy Spirit in effectual calling and identifies regeneration as the specific means by which it is accomplished.

Thomas Boston wrote, 'Effectual calling is the first entrance of a soul into the state of grace, the first step by which God's eternal purpose of love descends unto sinners, and we again ascend towards the glory to which we are chosen.' [38]

2. The Means of Effectual Calling

William Cunningham, the first Professor of Theology in the Free Church College in Edinburgh, in the first volume of his *Historical Theology*,[39] says

38. Thomas Boston, *Works*, Vol.1, pp.557,558.
39. William Cunningham, *Historical Theology*, Banner of Truth, 1979.

that there are three elements in the process by which individuals are brought to the place of salvation. Firstly, the gospel of the Lord Jesus Christ is made known to them; secondly, they are called upon to accept the offer of the gospel; then thirdly, the Holy Spirit enables individuals to accept the offer and respond to the invitation. It will be useful to look at each of these in turn.

Firstly, making the gospel known. This is one of the primary tasks of the Christian Church. In our capacity as ambassadors for Christ we must present to men and women the facts concerning Jesus Christ and then explain the significance of these facts for life and salvation. Nothing we might say about the supernatural work of God the Holy Spirit in any way diminishes the importance of this task. In response to our Saviour's command in Matthew 28:19-20 we are to go out and make disciples. There are many ways in which God might have made Christ known but, as 1 Corinthians 1:21 makes clear, he chose to do it by the preaching of his Word. Paul underlines this in Romans 10:17 where he tells us plainly that faith comes by hearing the message.

We are to take God's Word and bring it to bear upon the lives of men and women. We are to seek to persuade them of the truth of the gospel. This is a straightforward teaching function because it is when the truth of God is applied to the human mind that God begins to do his work. When Paul wrote to the Colossians he reminded them that they had heard the gospel and 'understood God's grace in all its truth' (Colossians 1:6). He goes on to say that they had 'learned' the gospel from Epaphras. To say (as some do) that the gospel is 'caught not taught' is not only a serious mistake, but might also be responsible for the absence of solid Bible teaching in much of what purports to be evangelism today. Our duty is to teach and preach God's Word. This is his designated method of bringing men and women to salvation.

Secondly, the call of the gospel. Having made the gospel known, the person doing so must invite his hearers to respond by looking to Christ for salvation. The gospel can never be simply an interesting story about past events. The very nature of the gospel demands a response. I am not suggesting that we must invite a response by asking people to walk to the front of a church at the end of a service, or to raise a hand as an indication of their response. In fact, that kind of invitation has often been counter-productive in that some people, having responded in such a way, imagine that they are Christians when in fact they have never known the regeneration of the Spirit. The call of the gospel which we are considering here is a general (or universal) call and is issued to every person without exception. It is clear from Scripture that in any situation and in any company we can issue the gospel offer: whoever believes in the Lord Jesus Christ will be saved (John 3:15-18).

Some people say that those who believe God to be sovereign in salvation cannot truly preach that unconditional offer of the gospel. How can you invite people to believe in the Lord Jesus Christ and be saved, they say, without knowing if they are predestined and if Christ has died for them? Indeed, in the late 17th and early 18th centuries this was a fierce issue of debate in Scotland. But to take such a view is to misunderstand the Reformed position.

I can go into any company of men and women at any time and issue that invitation to believe in the Lord Jesus Christ and I can accompany it with the promise that whoever does truly believe in Christ will be saved; and there is nothing in the doctrines of predestination or effectual calling which prevents such an invitation. Nevertheless, it is certainly true that a man or a woman will only be able to respond to that invitation if they are enabled so to do by the Holy Spirit.

Thirdly, the effectual call of the Spirit. It is clear from Scripture and also from our own experience that many of those who hear the call will not respond to it. Many hundreds of unbelievers hear the call of the gospel every day and yet do not respond to it. On the other hand, there are many who do respond and are saved. But there is a difficulty here: why is it that the same preacher, preaching the same Word, to the same group of people, perhaps from the same background, will find that some respond and some do not? Clearly, the difference is not in the preacher, or the sermon, or the circumstances in which the call is issued. Why is it, then, that some respond and some do not?

There are, of course, those who will say that the difference is simply one of choice. One individual freely chooses to believe and another chooses not to believe. Yet this interpretation cuts across the clear teaching of Scripture. How can someone who is spiritually dead choose to come alive? How can someone who is lost decide to be found? How can someone who is an enemy of God in his heart and mind choose to become a friend of God before anything has happened to effect a change in his sinful and rebellious heart? In any case, how can it truly be said that any human being has had free will since the Fall in Genesis 3?

The British author and preacher John Blanchard, speaking at the 'Keswick in Buckie' Convention in 1994, dealt with this notion that an individual was free to accept or reject the gospel entirely as they pleased. He asked us to imagine a young man who decides that he will be a Christian but, just to make it special, he decides that he will become a Christian on his birthday. So he holds a great party and on the stroke of 9pm (which he happened to know was the moment of his physical birth) he becomes a Christian and then announces this decision to the assembled company! The absurdity of that scenario helps to underpin this great doctrine of effectual calling. We are simply not free to act in this way. We can no more choose the place and time of our spiritual birth than we can choose the place and time of our natural birth. That is part of the implication of John 3. The same truth is emphasised elsewhere in the New Testament: 'No-one can come to me unless the Father who sent me draws him' (John 6:44); 'For many are invited but few are chosen' (Matthew 22:14).

How then does God actually bring his people to salvation? In Romans 1:16 Paul helps us by describing the gospel as the 'power of God for the salvation of everyone who believes'. Here is the answer: the gospel is not merely words, but in the case of those who believe it is the power of God for their salvation.

The very first sermon I ever heard on this subject was by James Philip. In it he used two stories from the New Testament in order to illustrate effectual calling. First, the story of the raising of Lazarus from the dead (John 11:43); second, the story of the man with the withered hand (Luke 6:10). In each case Jesus commanded the man to do precisely what he could not do. But the command contained within itself the power to enable the man to obey.

The gospel is the power of God at work, enabling men and women to do what they simply could not do in their own strength and power. They are enabled to respond to the gospel offer and are united to Christ.

Perhaps the verses which most clearly explain this doctrine of effectual calling are to be found in 2 Thessalonians 2:13,14:

> But we ought always to thank God for you, brothers loved by the Lord, because from the beginning God chose you to be saved through the sanctifying work of the Spirit and through belief in the truth. He called you to this through our gospel, that you might share in the glory of our Lord Jesus Christ.

Notice here that God chose them to be saved from the beginning but the means by which he effected this was the call of the gospel.

We can summarise this by saying that in the case of those whom God has chosen and for whom Christ died, the hearing of the gospel is accompanied by a moving of the Holy Spirit as a result of which they are born again.

3. The Place of Effectual Calling

We come now to consider the place of effectual calling. In other words, how does effectual calling relate to the other doctrines of grace? As we noted earlier, *The Westminster Confession of Faith*, in keeping with much Reformed theology in the 17th century, tends to treat effectual calling and regeneration as being the same thing. It is, however, important that we distinguish between them.

Louis Berkhof, the American theologian, makes

a distinction which is very helpful. He writes:

'It is a well known fact that in seventeenth century theology effectual calling and regeneration are often identified, or if not entirely identified, then at least in so far that regeneration is regarded as included in calling...

'In a systematic presentation of the truth, however, we should carefully discriminate between calling and regeneration.'[40]

The Princeton theologian A.A. Hodge helps us to understand:

'Regeneration is the effect produced by the Holy Spirit in effectual calling. The Holy Spirit, in the act of effectual calling, causes the soul to become regenerate by implanting a new governing principle or habit of spiritual affection and action. The soul itself, in conversion, immediately acts under the guidance of this new principle in turning from sin unto God through Christ.'[41]

We should also note that, in addition to regeneration, saving faith is bestowed upon us by God in our effectual calling. In this context, John Owen draws our attention to the connection between John

40. Louis Berkhof, *Systematic Theology*, Banner of Truth, 1971, pp. 470,471.
41. A. A. Hodge, *A Commentary on the Confession of Faith*, T. Nelson & Sons, 1870, pp.171,172.

6:29: 'The work of God is this: to believe in the one he has sent' and 6:44: 'No-one can come to me unless the Father who sent me draws him'. We might put it like this: There are two problems in every human being which need to be resolved. Firstly, our relationship with God needs to be restored; and secondly, our sinful nature needs to be changed. Effectual calling is the first step in the process which leads to these two objectives. Effectual calling and regeneration lead to saving faith. Faith leads on the one hand to justification and adoption (thus restoring a proper relationship with God); and on the other hand to repentance and sanctification (thus dealing with the sinful nature).

A fine balance is required in all of this. We have seen that effectual calling is a supernatural work of the Holy Spirit by which, in an instant, an individual is born again of the Holy Spirit and enabled to respond to the offer of the gospel. This, however, is not to deny that God can often prepare an individual for this moment by a prior work of the Holy Spirit in conviction of sin. Nor does this understanding of the matter deny the use of means, as for example, God's use of the Word in bringing someone to himself.

4. The Experience of Effectual Calling
In all of this we must be sure to emphasise the fact that God does not force us to accept the gospel against our will, rather he changes our will (Phil.

2:13) so that we accept the gospel willingly and gladly.

The Westminster Confession of Faith sums up the doctrine well, and highlights this very point:

All those whom God hath predestinated unto life, and those only, he is pleased, in his appointed and accepted time, effectually to call, by his word and Spirit, out of that state of sin and death in which they are by nature, to grace and salvation by Jesus Christ; enlightening their minds spiritually and savingly to understand the things of God; taking away their heart of stone, and giving unto them an heart of flesh; renewing their wills, and by his almighty power determining them to that which is good; and effectually drawing them to Jesus Christ; yet so as they come most freely, being made willing by his grace.' [42]

In one sense, the argument over whether or not grace is resistible is pointless. It is surely utterly inconceivable that anyone who has been enabled to see Christ in all his glory and to understand fully what has been accomplished on the cross at Calvary would then resist God's grace.

Perhaps the best way to draw all the threads of this teaching together is to turn our attention to a biblical example. There are several. We could look at the story of Paul's own conversion on the road to

---

42. Chapter 10, section 1.

Damascus (recorded in Acts 9), or the story of the Philippian jailor (recorded in Acts 16). But let us consider the story of Lydia in Acts 16:13-15. You will notice that the sequence of events is precisely as we would expect it on the basis of the biblical doctrine of effectual calling.

First, Paul and the others began to speak to the women who were there. Paul, we are told, had presented a message, and it is clear from verse 14 that this message demanded a response. Now here is the interesting point. Does it say that Lydia was persuaded by what she heard or that she was convinced by what Paul said? No! It says that 'the Lord opened her heart to respond to Paul's message'. Now clearly, from a human point of view, she was convinced, she was persuaded – but it was not the conviction itself which made her a Christian. It was the work of the Holy Spirit of God in opening her heart and enabling her to respond. So, then, there will always be these two sides: the divine call and the human persuasion.

If this truth about effectual calling is accepted, other passages of Scripture begin to make sense. For example, a few chapters earlier, in Acts 13 we find Paul and Barnabas preaching the gospel in Pisidian Antioch. In verse 48 of that chapter we read this, 'When the Gentiles heard this, they were glad and honoured the word of the Lord; and all who were appointed for eternal life believed.' We do not read here that it was all who 'decided' or all who were 'persuaded' but rather, all who were 'appointed'. Without a doctrine of effectual calling this verse is very difficult to understand. It must surely mean that in the case of those whom he had chosen for eternal life God worked effectually by his Spirit to grant them the gift of regeneration and faith and so bring them to salvation.

As Thomas Boston comments, 'The elect of God, in their natural condition, are lost sheep gone astray among the devil's goats; effectual calling is the bringing them out from among them, back to Christ's fold.' [43]

5. The Implications of Effectual Calling

The doctrine of effectual calling has several practical implications. Firstly, it should encourage us, especially during a period in the history of Christianity in this country when we are not seeing as many people being saved as in former days. If we are convinced that salvation is God's work then we will not despair.

Secondly, this doctrine should lead us to prayer. If salvation were to be accomplished by our gifts of persuasion and by the cleverness of our evangelistic methods then we could follow some of the hundred and one different suggestions which are forced upon us constantly. How many times have we been told that if we only follow this plan or that

43. Thomas Boston, *Works*, Vol.1, p.560.

scheme then our churches will be full in no time at all? But if we recognise that salvation comes by the effectual calling of God then we will *pray*. It also means that our evangelism will remain biblical rather than becoming more and more desperate, and descending into the depths of religious entertainment. Instead, it will continue to present Christ simply and powerfully.

Thirdly, it will encourage us to give all the glory to God. Souls will be saved and the gospel will be effective, but these results are not ours. How many times have we heard some of the evangelists of our day boasting about the number of people who have been converted or, more recently, boasting about the number of miracles they have seen. Where is the grace of God in all of that? It is the Lord who brings people to salvation, and all the glory must go to him.

All of this is summed up by Charles Wesley, who wrote these marvellous words:

Long my imprisoned spirit lay
fast bound in sin and nature's night;
Thine eye diffused a quickening ray,
I woke, the dungeon flamed with light;
My chains fell off, my heart was free,
I rose, went forth and followed thee.

In a nutshell, we can put it like this. The gospel is preached to a congregation of men and women.

Some of them have heard the message many times. But then something happens. The 'quickening ray' is diffused, the chains of sin and spiritual death are destroyed and a man or a woman, newly converted, goes forth to follow Christ. What has happened? The Holy Spirit has accompanied the outward call of the gospel with an effectual call, and one more sinner has been brought into the kingdom of God.

Chapter 15

OUR RESPONSE

All along, I have been assuming that those reading this book will be Christians, perhaps fairly new in the faith. But this may not always be the case. If at this point you are not yet a Christian then let me urge you to become one. I remember listening to my friend Philip Hair preaching at a mission in Strathclyde University in which we were both involved. Towards the end of the mission he placed great emphasis upon the fact that Jesus of Nazareth claimed to be God. If this claim was true, he said, then it forces us to make a response. I believe that he was absolutely right to centre in on that great fact.

In other words, when you are faced with Jesus Christ and his claims upon your life, it is necessary to make a decision. That decision ought to be 'yes' or 'no'. But there are some who put off the decision and they say, 'perhaps later'. My task is to encourage you to say 'yes' to Jesus and to show the dangers of delaying the decision.

In Mark 15:16-32, a passage describing the events at the time of the crucifixion of Jesus, we are introduced to a number of people, and their reactions to Jesus. Let us look at some of them.

The Soldiers

Verses 16-20 describe how the soldiers mocked, jeered and taunted the Lord. We also have a description of the violence which he suffered at their hands. They dressed him like a king or an emperor and pretended to worship him, and then they beat him. You might imagine that these were hardened men and that the person of Jesus could make no impact on them. But this is not so. In verse 39 we find this: 'And when the centurion, who stood there in front of Jesus, heard his cry and saw how he died, he said, "Surely this man was the Son of God!"' A tough Roman soldier, he had no doubt crucified many people, but when he witnessed the death of this man he knew that he was different. Tradition has it that this soldier became a Christian, but whether or not this is true, it is certainly the case that the death of Jesus had a marked effect upon him, and convinced him that Jesus was the Son of God.

Matthew's version of the story tells us that it was not only the centurion who was affected by the death of Christ, but the common soldiers too, those very men who had taunted and beaten him. In Matthew 27:54 we are told that they joined with the centurion in confessing Jesus' sonship. One thing is clear. This was no ordinary crucifixion, and that could be seen even by those soldiers. God revealed himself on that day in a powerful way.

Simon of Cyrene

The next person we encounter in this chapter is Simon of Cyrene, the father of Alexander and Rufus (verse 21). We are told that he was 'forced' to carry the cross of Jesus. Indeed, Luke tells us (23:26) that he was 'seized' for this very purpose. The whole tenor of these verses suggests a man who was unwilling and unhappy. Once again, however, there are good reasons for believing that he later became a Christian, no doubt because of the effect that Jesus had upon him. In Acts 13:1 we are told of a Simon called Niger who was one of the prophets and teachers in the church at Antioch – and many scholars believe that this is the same man who carried the cross. Also, in Romans 16:13 we hear Paul speak of 'Rufus, chosen in the Lord, and his mother, who has been a mother to me too' and many believe that this speaks of Simon's wife and son. Whether these suggestions are true or not is difficult to say, but it seems a reasonable possibility that Simon later became a Christian. There is certainly a strong historical tradition to that effect.

The Two Robbers

In verses 27 and 32 we read of the two robbers who were crucified with Jesus. In particular, in verse 32 we read, 'Those crucified with him also heaped insults on him.' But this was not the end of the story, because one of those robbers began to take a different line. In Luke 23:39-43 we learn that one of the robbers rebuked the other and asked Jesus to remember him when he came into his kingdom. Jesus assured the man that he would be in paradise that very day. Even on the cross, while he was suffering the agony of one of the most cruel and painful methods of execution ever invented, Jesus took time to assure that robber of salvation.

The Others

But there were many who were apparently left unaffected by the death of Jesus and who, right up until the end, gave no sign of being moved or changed or converted. There were the passers-by of whom we read in verses 29-30. They hurled insults at him and urged him to come down from the cross if he was as powerful as he had claimed to be. The paradox is that Jesus *could* have come down from the cross, but he chose to remain there and die for the salvation of others.

Then there were the chief priests and the teachers of the law (verses 31-32). These were his implacable enemies, those who had from the earliest days of his public ministry sought his death. The very words they used demonstrated that they had completely misunderstood him. For example, they said, 'He saved others but he can't save himself!' (verse 31). They could not see that it was in the very act of dying that he did save others. Then they added, 'Let this Christ, this King of Israel, come down now from the cross, that we may see and believe' (verse 32). But even had he done so it would not have made any difference! They had seen Jesus heal the sick and raise the dead. He had fed the 5,000 and walked on the water. There was no shortage of miracles and another would have been dismissed in just the same way as earlier ones. The simple fact is that they hated Jesus. Their hearts were closed to him.

Jesus once told a parable of an unconverted rich man who died, and when he realised the terrible fate awaiting others like himself, he wanted someone to go and warn his family (Luke 16:19-31). In response, he was told that they had Moses and the prophets and should listen to them. The rich man insisted that they would definitely listen if someone returned from the dead, but he was told in no uncertain terms that they would not believe even if this were to happen.

This has implications for today. The biblical way of evangelism is not one which insists on the need for miracles and so on. That was the method which Jesus specifically disavowed both in the parable and when the devil tempted him to perform miracles so that people would believe in him (Matthew 4:1-11). If people's hearts are set against the gospel and against Christ, then until their hearts are opened by the Holy Spirit of God and they themselves are enabled to see Jesus as Saviour and Lord, they will not believe. All the miracles in the world will not change that.

What then do we find in this chapter? We find a Roman centurion and other soldiers declaring that Jesus was the Son of God, because of the way in which he died and the events surrounding his death. We find mockery and violence changed to fear and confession of faith. We find a man seized and forced to carry the cross of Jesus becoming, as far as we can determine, a disciple – and his family also. We find two robbers taunting Jesus as they were cruci-fied with him – and then one being changed by the power of God and promised a place in Paradise. We find some passers-by and some Jewish religious leaders who were unrelenting in their hatred, and who showed by their words that they had failed either to recognise Jesus or to understand his purpose.

In this passage, then, we find some people who said 'yes' to Jesus and some who said 'no'. We could, of course, mention many others. You don't have to read very much of the New Testament to come across people who said 'yes' to Jesus when they met him, for example, Zacchaeus. And there are many others who said 'no', for example, the rich young ruler, whose money was more impor-tant to him than following Jesus.

These people came face to face with Jesus and made a clear decision, either for or against. But what about those who try to delay the decision?

In Luke 14:15-24 Jesus told a parable. He said that a man was preparing a banquet and sent out invitations. But the people who received the invitations made excuses and said they couldn't come. No doubt many of them would have liked to attend the banquet, but there were other things which stopped them. Many of the things which stopped them were good things, but even good things become evil when they act as a barrier between the sinner and God.

Again, in Luke 9:59-62, Jesus asked people to follow him. One man said, 'Lord, first let me go and bury my father' (verse 59). The other said, 'First let me go back and say goodbye to my family' (verse 61). In both cases Jesus insisted that they should follow him immediately and without attending to these other matters. This might seem very harsh to us, but Jesus could look into their hearts and perhaps he knew that they were trying to delay the decision, trying to put him off. They wanted to follow but it was not their immediate priority.

There are many people like that today. I have met some who say, 'I'll think about Christianity when I'm old and I've enjoyed life', and others who say, 'Perhaps later, when I've had time to build a career and a family and I'm ready to settle down'. But that kind of procrastination is folly because we do not know what tomorrow holds.

Jesus still meets people
The remarkable thing about Christianity is that Jesus of Nazareth still confronts people today. We might have thought that the people about whom

we read in Mark 15 were the last to be confronted by Christ, but this is not the case. What about Paul, or Lydia or the Philippian jailor? These were all confronted with the claims of Christ long after his death. Jesus continues to confront us with his claims. Even today people's lives are being changed by this man who rose again from the dead and is alive for evermore.

That the death of one man 2,000 years ago should continue to change people's lives after he died is almost beyond belief to some people, and yet it is true.

Think of John Newton, a slave trader, who met Jesus and was born again of the Spirit of God and bore witness to his conversion in the hymn *Amazing Grace*.

Think of Charles Colson, one of President Nixon's men, who was convicted of various criminal offences following the Watergate scandal, but who then met Jesus, was born again of the Spirit of God, and now spends his life visiting prisons to speak to the prisoners about Christ, his death upon the cross, and the hope of eternal life.

Think of Nicky Cruz whose story was told in the book *The Cross and the Switchblade*. He was a gang leader in New York City, involved in violence and murder, but someone took time to tell him about Christ – at considerable personal risk – and ultimately he was born again of the Spirit of God and was called into a worldwide evangelistic ministry.

Many ordinary people I have known also come
to mind as I write. I think of a womanising drunk-
ard who had no interest whatsoever in the Christian faith until one day God stopped him in his
tracks, and he saw the significance of the cross,
and believed. His changed life was a powerful testimony to the grace of God. Sadly he died only a
couple of years after this, but he was ready to die,
and many were challenged by the manner of his
dying.

I think of a young unmarried woman who was
living with a man by whom she had had a child.
The party and the pub were what their lives were
centred around. That young woman became a Christian and is serving God in her home and in her vil-
lage. Now married, her husband can't understand
the change in her life and as yet doesn't like it too
much, but her transformed life is a powerful testimony to the truth.

I think of a man who came the way of the cross
in his youth. He had been a wild man, fighting,
drinking and so on. But he met with Jesus and was
changed. For about the next 25 years he lived as a
Christian, faithful and strong. His wife hated the
Christian church and all that it stood for, and hated
it when he went out to speak or preach. A few years
ago that man died, and two months later his wife
met Jesus, understood the significance of the cross,
and she began to serve God – although there was
grief in her heart for the years which were lost in

many ways because she did not share with her husband the most important thing in his life – his Christian faith.

We should also remember that it is not only those who have lived 'bad' lives who need to be born again. I can think of a woman who lived a good life, whose job involved her in service to the community. She was well-known and well-liked. She attended church and to every outward appearance was a Christian. But one day she testified that she had become a Christian. Up until that point she had merely been going through the motions. Suddenly it was real!

As we come to the end of this book I want to ask you where you stand in all of this. Have you been changed through an encounter with this man Jesus who died on the cross at Calvary? Have you been looking for some purpose in life? Do you feel that life is pointless? Do you feel burdened down with cares and worries, not knowing where to turn? Have you been attending church for a long time but always felt that there was something missing, that somehow you haven't really found the answer?

Whoever you are, if you are not a believer, then come to the risen Christ for salvation. Remember the words of Jesus to Nicodemus, 'You must be born again.'

Study Questions

The following questions are designed to point readers to the central themes of each chapter of the book. If you are not sure of the answers to these questions then perhaps you should read the relevant chapter again!

Chapter 1

Does the description of the author's experience reflect your own experience?

Is the need for new birth preached and explained in your church?

Chapter 2

Why is new birth necessary?

What was the 'Fall'?

What is God's attitude towards sin?

Chapter 3

Give a definition of the word 'Christian'.

Why is the story of Nicodemus so important?

What is the 'Baptism with the Holy Spirit'?

Chapter 4

How can we be 'right with God'?

Define the word 'justification'.

If God is just and holy, how can he forgive sin?

Chapter 5

Is every human being a child of God?

What is the significance of the Christian doctrine of adoption?

How do we become the children of God?

Chapter 6

Why did John the Baptist call Jesus the 'Lamb of God'?

Why is it important that Jesus was man as well as being God?

What is the relationship between Adam and Christ?

Chapter 7

What does the word 'holy' mean?

Is God holy?

Is it possible for human beings to be holy?

Chapter 8

Does new birth always lead to new life?

What is the connection between faith and action?

Summarise the two aspects of sanctification.

Chapter 9

What is 'mortification'?

If we are Christians, why do we still sin?

What part does obedience play in spiritual growth?

Chapter 10

What is spiritual warfare?

Describe the armour which God gives us.

In what sense is the Word of God a 'sword'?

Chapter 11

What are 'neonomians' and 'antinomians'?

What was the error of 'perfectionism'?

Is spiritual victory a possibility or a certainty?

Chapter 12

Is holiness a condition of salvation or is salvation unconditional?

Is holiness essential for salvation?

What is the connection between holiness and heaven?

Chapter 13

What does Paul mean when he speaks of those God 'foreknew'?

Is regeneration the same as conversion?

What is the connection between regeneration and justification?

Chapter 14

What does 'called' mean in Romans 8:30?

Is the call of the gospel the same as the 'effectual call'?

What is the connection between predestination and effectual calling?

Chapter 15

Have you encountered the living Lord Jesus Christ?

Have you been born again?

Dr. Andrew McGowan has been Director of the Highland Theological Institute, Elgin since its inception in 1994. A graduate of Aberdeen University and of the Union Theological Seminary, New York, Andrew is a minister of the Church of Scotland and served as a parish minister for 14 years before taking up his present appointment. He has contributed a number of theological and historical articles to various Dictionaries including *The New Dictionary of Theology* (IVP), *The Encyclopaedia of the Reformed Faith* (Westminster/John Knox Press), the *Dictionary of Scottish Church History and Theology* (T & T Clark), and the *New Dictionary of National Biography* (Oxford University Press). His doctoral thesis, *The Federal Theology of Thomas Boston*, will be published by Paternoster Press in 1996. Andrew is married to June and they have three sons.